Sure Hands
Strong Heart

Sure Hands
Strong Heart

The Life of
Daniel Hale Williams

Lillie Patterson

SILVER BURDETT GINN

SURE HANDS, STRONG HEART:
The Life of Daniel Hale Williams

Copyright © 1981 by Abingdon
All Rights Reserved

Library of Congress Cataloging in Publication Data
PATTERSON, LILLIE.
Sure hands, strong heart.
Bibliography: p.
Summary: A biography of the black surgeon who, among other achievements, was the first to perform open heart surgery.
1. Williams, Daniel Hale, 1856-1931—Juvenile literature. 2. Afro-American surgeons—Biography—Juvenile literature. 3. Surgeons—United States—Biography—Juvenile literature. [1. Williams, Daniel Hale, 1856–1931. 2. Afro-Americans—Biography. 3. Physicians]
I. Title.
RD27.35.W54P37   617'.092'4 [B] [92]   81-2660   AACR2

ISBN 0-382-33766-2

To honor black physicians whose contributions to the advancement of modern medicine have often been unheralded or unknown

Acknowledgments

The author wishes to acknowledge with appreciation the work and dedication of Helen Buckler, whose painstaking research into the life and geneology of Daniel Hale Williams laid a firm foundation upon which other scholars might build. The gift of the Daniel Hale Williams Collection to Howard University makes it possible for other researchers to benefit from her research notes, clippings, photographs, photostats, and correspondence, assembled during the writing of *Doctor Dan: Pioneer in American Surgery,* later revised as *Daniel Hale Williams, Negro Surgeon.* (Pitman Publishing Corporation, 1954, 1968)

Special thanks are also given to the staff of the Moorland-Spingarn Research Center, Howard University, for assistance in using the Daniel Hale Williams Collection, and to the staff of countless other libraries consulted during the preparation of this biography.

Contents

CHAPTER 1

A Time of Movement

Movement.

The time was one of movement, of change. It was a time for dreaming daring dreams, and for whistling bold songs.

A time for feeling free.

Daniel Hale Williams whistled a free-feeling tune with the joy of being a nine-year-old on a day in June. He sauntered along the new brick sidewalks that led to the business section of Hollidaysburg, Pennsylvania.

Hollidaysburg nestled in the valley of the Juanita River. The town formed the connecting point of the Pennsylvania State Canal and the Portage Railroad. The boom town mirrored the restless busy period of the middle and later 1860s.

Dan's lively eyes took in the hustle and bustle around him. Stage coaches and covered wagons clattered along the dusty streets. Men stepped along with purposeful strides. Saddled horses stomped restlessly beside the hitching posts that lined the thoroughfares.

The boy quickened his pace to match the movements of the crowd. When he came to the town square, known as the Diamond, he stopped.

He had reached the heart of the business district—the main shops, the opera house, the courthouse.

He turned into one of the shops, a two-story brick building. A sign posted at the second floor windows advertised a photographer's shop. With a quick dart Dan turned and ran through the door to the first floor rooms.

This was his father's world. The elder Daniel Hale Williams was part of the growth and progress of Hollidaysburg. His barbershop was the biggest in town. He had purchased property and invested in land rich in iron ore. Townspeople knew him as a shrewd businessman, and the leader of the small group of black citizens.

Young Dan and his father greeted each other with smiles. No words were needed between them. The son stood quietly beside the barber chair while his father finished trimming the blond hair of the customer. Only after the customer had paid and left did Dan begin a conversation.

"I came to help you," he began.

"Good," his father answered as he tousled Dan's red hair. "The last months have been busier than usual. It seems that the whole world is passing through Hollidaysburg these days."

The June sun beamed into the room and highlighted the features of the two faces. One face seemed a carbon copy of the other. Dan had inherited his father's curving, sensitive mouth and deep-set brown eyes. His red hair, more burnished

than his father's, curled around his forehead in the same manner.

Another customer walked in and Dan set to work. Every inch of the barbershop was a world of exploration for him. With slow precision he folded stacks of white towels and placed them within easy reach of his father's hands. He lined up containers of hair tonic, savoring the aroma of each jar or bottle.

Customers came and went. Dan washed the tools, swept and dusted, and straightened the chairs.

"My boy is going to be a great barber one day," his father encouraged.

Dan's wide smile brought out the dimples in his cheeks. "When can I start?"

"Soon." His father's voice grew serious. "Very soon now I will start teaching you."

I'll learn to be a barber.

With these words singing a refrain in his mind, Dan left the barbershop for home. As always he took the route that wound past the canal.

Here was another world that intrigued young Dan. He never tired of studying the flurry of action along the busy canal. The man-made waterway formed a link in the transportation chain taking pioneers across the Allegheny Mountains to the newly-opened regions in the West.

Everything along the canal seemed to be moving, moving, moving. The Civil War had ended.

Fighting men were free to return home, or move on to seek new ventures.

The nation was free of the slave system. Black families, ex-slaves and freeborn, could move about unmolested.

Pioneers had opened up more territories for farming and living. The United States was free to move forward, to stretch and grow.

The life along the canal reflected the moving-ahead time in America. Families crowded their household goods and livestock aboard the canal barges. Children followed their parents, hugging pets and lugging bundles of clothing. The loaded barges began another leg of their journey to the West.

The West!

The very term conjured up adventure to many who heard it. Dan was no different. He left the canal and headed for home. In the distance he could see the familiar wall of granite known as Chimney Rocks, part of the Allegheny Mountains. What mysteries lay beyond those mountains? Why were so many people moving?

Such questions pursued Dan as he entered the third and most important of his worlds—his home. He skipped up the steps of their frame house on Blair Street. This solid two-story square house had been home since he was born there on January 18, 1856.

The house was quiet except for the whirring of his

15

mother's sewing machine. Dan tiptoed behind her chair and stood watching her work.

Sarah Price Williams greeted her son with a nod, never breaking the rhythm of her stitching. Dan's eyes followed the yellow muslin as she sewed white lace around the edges. The bright colors blended beautifully against his mother's coppery skin and raven-black hair.

"Who gets a new dress this time?" he asked, gently fingering the yellow material.

"Sally," his mother answered. "She is growing up and hates to wear Ann's old clothes."

Dan's mother folded the dress. "Bring some wood for the fire," she told him. "Aunt Mary Jane is here for a visit."

"Aunt Mary Jane!" Dan's voice squeaked two octaves higher. "Where is she now?"

"She is worn out from her trip and sleeping now. Don't wake her." His mother went to the kitchen and quietly began preparing dinner.

Aunt Mary Jane was the wife of Dan's beloved uncle, Henry Price, who had died three years before at the age of forty-eight. Uncle Henry was the most glamorous man Dan had ever known. Each time he came to visit he brought his big guitar strapped to his saddle bag. He, too, had been a barber. He also had his own string band.

Dan stacked sticks of wood in the box in the kitchen, moving quietly so as not to awaken their guest. Later, he stood in the front yard to watch for his father.

Daniel Williams II came striding down Blair Street slender and erect as an Indian chief. By the time he came in the house Aunt Mary Jane was awake. For a full five minutes everyone in the family was caught up in a round of hugging and kissing. Their aunt was younger than Uncle Henry had been, and very pretty.

After supper they moved to the parlor, the room set aside for company. The grownups sat on the overstuffed chairs and the young people squeezed together on the sofa and on chairs from the kitchen.

The light from the oil lamps flickered across their faces, playing up the varied shadings that revealed the melting-pot mixture of their family heritage.

Eighteen-year-old Henry Price, the oldest boy, was named for his mother's father. He was short and stocky. Price, as his family called him, had the straight black hair and bronze coloring of his mother's Indian ancestors.

So did his sixteen-year-old sister, Sarah. Everyone called her Sally.

Ann Effine, the oldest girl, was nineteen. She was fair and red headed like her father's German and Irish forebears.

The three youngest girls sat primly in their dressed-up clothes. Ida was twelve, Alice Price was eight, and Florence May was six. Each of the pretty

17

girls showed mixed strains of their Indian-German-Irish-Black American ancestry.

Whenever the Price and Williams family came together they loved to talk. And the talk usually turned to their family history.

They asked Mary Price about her business in Harrisburg.

"Business is very good," she told them. "I have customers from as far away as Seattle, Washington."

After Uncle Henry's death his wife had kept the barbershop and had studied to learn the hairdressing trade. M. J. Price & Son, Wigmakers, was a thriving business in the capital city of Pennsylvania.

The family recalled Uncle Henry's love for music. "He was a musical genius," his sister reminisced. "He could glance at a sheet of music, or hear a tune, and later play it perfectly, note for note."

"Uncle Henry taught me to play the guitar," Price spoke up.

"He taught me the strings too," Dan chimed in.

Grandfather Price of Annapolis, Maryland, was another favorite topic of their storytelling. "Your grandfather was one of the best preachers in Maryland," their mother boasted. "Most of the Price men were great barbers, or preachers, or musicians. Some were all three."

Daniel Williams II, in his quiet, serious tones, recalled stories of his Scottish grandmother, his German great-grandfather, and his Afro-American father. "Our ancestors helped to settle this area," he reflected. "The Williamses have lived in Pennsylvania since the early 1700s."

He told the children how his father, Daniel Williams I, had followed the Juanita River, just as the Holliday brothers had done. Adam and William Holliday, struck by the beauty of the valley, staked out large farms. From this beginning the town named in their honor began to grow. Daniel Williams I had followed the river and settled near it with his Scotch-Irish wife. He ran a barbershop weekdays and preached on Sundays.

The storytelling suddenly shifted.

"Tell us about the slave," Ida begged.

These storytelling sessions never ended without one of the little girls asking for this tale. Sally told it now. She had been old enough to remember all the details.

It happened during the days of slavery. Hollidaysburg was an important station along the Underground Railroad. The townspeople would hide the slaves until they could whisk them away to Canada and freedom. One night a fugitive slave slipped into town. Word reached the people that his owner was on the way to get him. Worse, rumors said that Southern troops were coming to Hollidaysburg.

A black man, risking his life, took the runaway and hid him in Chimney Rocks. The townsfolk knew he was there, and trembled at the thought of the poor slave alone in the mountains. They also trembled at the thought of the troops.

Finally, the conductors of the Underground Railroad were able to smuggle the slave out of town and away to freedom. But each time the small children looked up at Chimney Rocks, they shivered at the thought of the story.

The storytelling went on. In the tradition of countless black families, the history and traditions were being passed along by word of mouth. This was important, and the children knew it. Achievements, hardships, talents, even misdeeds of family members made fodder for the shaping of young minds.

The night, the stories, all sent sparks of exciting ideas shooting through young Dan's mind. Before he went to bed, he took one last lingering look at Chimney Rocks, made visible by the light of a bright moon. He went to sleep, his mind spinning with fanciful imaginings.

CHAPTER 2
A Time of Change

"Moving? Did you say we are moving?" Dan stopped sweeping the barbershop and stared at his father. "Moving where?"

His father took the broom from his tight grip and led him over to a chair. "Yes, son. We are going South to visit Grandmother Price in Annapolis."

Sensing Dan's surprise and fears at this sudden news, his father talked quietly about their plans. The barbershop would be leased to another businessman. The family house would be rented. An attorney, a close friend of the family, would handle all the details.

"What about the girls?" Dan asked. "Is everyone going?"

"Everyone is going," Daniel Williams assured him. "We will . . ." Suddenly he doubled over in a spasm of coughing.

Dan stood over him, patting his back until the coughing eased. "You have that cold again," he worried.

His father nodded. "This is another reason for our going to Annapolis. The rest should help me cure it."

The two stayed in the barbershop talking until the

late afternoon sun began to fade behind the mountains. There was still another reason for going to Maryland, Dan's father confessed. "This will give me more time to work with the National Equal Rights League," he said. "We hope to establish new branches in other states." The League had been organized to push for freedom and full citizenship for all people of color. Daniel Williams, one of the sponsors, had worked with it from the time of its founding.

"Freedom from bondage has been won." He looked directly into Dan's eyes. "The real fight is only now beginning. I cannot rest until every person in this land is given equal rights."

Dan slipped his hands into his father's and their fingers interlocked in understanding.

Over the next few days the excitement of the other members of the family put Dan in the mood for traveling. None of the children had ever been South. It was not until now—now that slavery had ended—that nonwhite families could travel everywhere at will. Before this, they were forced to carry passes, or "free papers," to prove they were not runaway slaves. And even then, there was always the fear of being captured and sold into bondage. With the new freedom of movement, families were locating and visiting kinfolk in hopes of reestablishing old ties.

On a day near the end of 1865, the Williams family arrived in Annapolis. Dan fell in love with

Grandmother Ann Price at first sight. She lived in a big house near historic Church Circle, within calling distance of the domed Statehouse, Maryland's Capitol. Annapolis had no segregated housing pattern. Enterprising free black men, such as Dan's grandfather, had bought valuable property in prime locations.

One of the first things their father did was to enroll the children in school. The Stanton School was new. It was supervised by the Freedmen's Bureau, Daniel II informed his children. They already knew about the Bureau, the agency set up by the United States Government to help the ex-slaves obtain schooling, health care, and legal protection.

"Get all the education you can," Daniel Williams preached to his children. "We colored people must cultivate the mind."

All who knew him were familiar with this challenge, and with the intense look on his face when he said the words. Young Dan was no exception. At the new school he took to his books with a new zest for study. He liked his teacher, and he liked the friends he made there. His best friend was Hutchins Bishop, son of a prominent family. "I'll show you the city," Dan's new friend offered.

There was a lot to show. Annapolis lacked the boomtown atmosphere of Hollidaysburg, but it had retained the charm and grandeur of colonial days.

History was Dan's favorite subject and the city offered on-the-spot lessons.

The two boys strolled along the narrow cobbled streets and studied the grand colonial homes, marked by their huge chimneys. They stood on the wharves, watching the boats—sailboats, skipjacks, sloops, bugeyes, schooners. Sometimes they took their lines and fished from the docks.

On other days they went past the United States Naval Academy in hopes of seeing the midshipmen in their precision drills. From the Academy they walked to St. John's College to see the overspreading tulip poplar known as the "Liberty Tree". It was over five hundred years old, Dan's friend boasted. Beneath its branches, Indian treaties had been signed, and men had met to plot the American Revolution.

Dan visited the historic churches of Annapolis. He viewed the tall spires of old St. Anne's on Church Circle. He attended services in the Asbury Methodist Episcopal Church where his Grandfather Price had preached. His grandfather had donated the land on which the church was built.

While Dan's schoolmate introduced him to the history of the city, his grandmother taught him the history of the Price family. She loved to talk, and Dan was a good listener. Grandmother Ann Wilks Price described her life growing up as a slave in Maryland. She lived on the same plantation with Frederick Douglass. The two were cousins. Dan knew about Douglass, for his name was frequently in the news. He had read how Douglass made a daring escape from a slave plantation and later became a famous orator and abolitionist.

One question puzzled Dan. Frederick Douglass had run away from slavery. "How did you get free?" he asked his grandmother.

"Your grandfather bought me," she said softly. Grandfather Henry Price had worked hard, she told Dan. He had saved his money and invested in stocks and real estate. The money from his investments went toward buying slaves so that he could set them free.

She took her grandchildren to St. Anne's Churchyard to see the inscription written on Grandfather Price's gravestone.

Sacred to the memory of REVEREND HENRY PRICE who died in Annapolis February 20, 1863 in the 71st year of his age. By Faith he lived on earth, in Hope he died, by Love he lives in Heaven.

The children saw less and less of their father. He was on the go, traveling and speaking for the Equal Rights League. "Schooling!" he preached to his audiences. "Schooling for young and old. Our race must progress, but we can do it only if we educate our children."

The idea of education for his race became a crusade for the gentle barber. He urged parents to organize day schools and night schools and learn from one another. "We utterly fail in our duty to our children if we neglect to give them education," he said. "Far better it is for us to do with plainer food and less finery and carefully cultivate the minds of those who must take our places."

Each time he returned home from a trip his family noticed that he was coughing more. They pleaded with him to go to bed and rest. He refused. There was too much to be done, he told them.

The early months of 1867 turned bitterly cold. One day he came home from one of his trips and collapsed. His children were told the sad news. Their father had developed quick tuberculosis, known by the dreaded name, "galloping consumption." The disease advanced rapidly. Through the dark winter days it sapped his strength and weakened his body.

Springtime came and spruced up the city, but it brought no hope to the sorrowful household. Daniel Williams II died on a Sunday in May of that year 1867. They buried him in the Price family plot of St. Anne's Churchyard.

Young Dan's happy, secure world was suddenly shattered. Nothing would ever be the same again. He could sense it. He grew silent and withdrawn.

His mother, distraught and brokenhearted, could not cope with the turn of events. Her husband had always handled all business matters. She had grown up sheltered and had married at the age of fifteen. She lacked the experience to manage the property and investments he left.

Price, the oldest boy, took his fate into his own hands. He decided to go and live with cousins in New York so that he could study law.

Sally and Ann were invited by some of their father's cousins to come and live in Illinois. There were wonderful opportunities for training in the hair goods trade, the cousins wrote.

Their mother gave her consent for them to go. She did more. She decided to go along with them. Perhaps she, too, would learn the art of hairdressing as Mary Jane Price had done.

The family would have to split up. Ida and Alice were enrolled in St. Frances' Academy, an expensive Catholic boarding school in Baltimore City. Florence, the youngest, would stay with Grandmother Price.

That left Dan. Poor Dan. His mother took his hands and explained that Mr. Mason, an old family friend, ran a small training school at his home in Baltimore. "You will live with him and learn the shoemaking trade," she said.

Shoemaking! The word sounded alien to Dan's ears.

His world toppled completely. His happy, carefree, musical, story-loving family would be scattered, splintered this way and that. They would never be put back together again as the beautiful unit they had been.

While the other family members packed in eagerness, Dan became more morose and sullen. He went about unsmiling, locking his sad thoughts behind a wall of silent withdrawal.

CHAPTER 3

On His Own

Dan woke to the strident cries of the street sellers. He did not like shoemaking, but there were many things he found fascinating in the port city of Baltimore.

He liked the early-morning street vendors, jingling their bells and blowing small horns. Ice was not yet in general use and housewives needed the food products of these door-to-door salesmen.

Dan's ears, so attuned to music, picked out the rhythm of the fish peddler. "Fish, fish. Get your fresh fish."

From a nearby alley a clam man echoed with his sing-song call. "Fresh sand-y coo-lams! Fresh sand-y coo-lams!"

The songs of the peddlers brought Dan alert and ready to face another day of work as a shoemaker's apprentice. The head of "Mr. Mason's Training School for Boys" was Mr. C. M. C. Mason. He was proud of his students, and the work he was doing to train them for skilled jobs. The school was set up in several rooms of his home.

Dan was fond of Mr. Mason, but simply could not force himself to like shoemaking. The strong smell of the hides made him ill. He hated the long hours of sitting on a bench sewing on tough leather. It was a good trade. Dan knew this. Shoes and boots were in great demand. But Dan also knew that the trade was not for him.

Somehow he had to escape. As surely as his cousin Frederick Douglass had escaped from slavery, he had to find a way of freeing himself from a bondage that enslaved his spirit.

The chance came one day. Mr. Mason left to buy leather for shoes. Dan sat quietly working, keeping his thoughts to himself. When the time came to break for lunch, he slipped out the door.

Run, Dan. His mind urged his feet down the cobbled streets. Run past the new brick homes with their gleaming white steps. Run faster than the street cars pulled by high-stepping horses. Dan did not stop running until he arrived out of breath at the railway station.

He searched until he found the railway agent. He knew that the agent and Daniel Williams II had been friends.

"Please," Dan gasped in a breathless voice. "Please help me. I need a pass to go to my mother in Illinois."

The agent could read the desperate unhappiness in the pale face, so like that of his dead friend. After several minutes of questioning and thinking, he agreed to give Dan a railroad pass.

Dan took the slip of paper, his passport to a

future in the West. At the age of twelve he was on his own.

The train wheels clicked off the miles to Rockford, Illinois. Dan reached his cousin's home tired and hungry. What would his mother say when she saw him? Would she send him back by the next train? Dan rapped on the door, shivering with weariness and apprehension.

His mother answered the knock. Wordlessly, Dan pleaded with his eyes. He held out both hands toward her.

Sarah Price Williams stared at her son in disbelief. "How did you get to Rockford?" she asked.

"The train," Dan whispered.

At this simple answer his mother hugged him hard. Her lighthearted laughter let Dan know that she would not scold him. His spirits lifted.

"Let me stay in Rockford with you," he implored. "I can take care of myself."

She hugged him again. "I'll let you stay. If you have enough spunk to come from Maryland to Illinois and find me, you have enough spunk to take care of yourself."

The Midwest had a welcome for anyone with spunk. Most of the frontier towns had not yet put up rigid racial barriers. A person was judged by his worth, not by his skin coloring. Everyone was free to chart his own career, to blaze his own trail.

Dan began to blaze his own trail. His sister Sally

helped him find the nearest school, a one-room building that stayed open a few months each year. Sally and Ann were both learning the hairdressing trade.

Along with his schooling, Dan found part-time work. He had learned so much about barbering from his father that he made a fine barber's apprentice. Once again Dan began to feel happy and secure.

The feeling did not last long. His mother became restless again. She was homesick to see her younger daughters and her mother. As suddenly as she had decided to come to Illinois she made up her mind to return to Annapolis.

Dan was free to go or stay, she told him. He could remain with Sally in Illinois. Or, he could return with her to Annapolis.

He chose the Midwest. His mother returned to Maryland, taking Ann with her. Over the next few years he boarded in the home of first one Williams cousin, then another. He always managed to make enough money to pay for his keep.

One summer he took a job aboard a lake steamer. Life in the Midwest had shown him the joy of boating, swimming, and fishing. He saved up his money and bought a guitar. Remembering the basic chords his uncle had taught him, he soon learned to play the popular shanty ballads. On the long boat rides he entertained travelers by playing his guitar and singing. Music helped to fill the void left by his father's death and the breakup of his family.

When Dan was sixteen, Sally decided to move to the town of Edgerton, Wisconsin. She had become an expert in making fancy hair pieces that were fashionable with women. Dan moved with her, and this time opened his own barbershop.

The town was beautiful. The people were friendly. There was one drawback, however. Edgerton did not have a school for him to attend. So Dan began to look around for a place that had a large barbershop in which he could work, and a high school in which he could study.

He found this combination in nearby Janesville, Wisconsin, a thriving town of more than ten thousand people. It not only boasted a barbershop, but the barbershop was owned by a black man.

One afternoon Dan dressed in his best clothes and went to Janesville to talk with this barber. He could read the impressive sign above the barbershop long before he reached the building: "Harry Anderson's Tonsorial Parlor and Bathing Rooms."

The owner, a solidly built man with a wide grin, greeted him. "I am Charles Henry Anderson," he said, gripping Dan's hand firmly. "Everyone around here calls me Harry."

"I am Daniel Hale Williams, sir. I understand you can use an extra barber."

The two sized each other up. Harry Anderson sported a well-trimmed beard, and short cropped hair that crinkled in small curls above a high forehead. His skin had the ruddy glow of a healthy man who spent hours outdoors.

Dan had grown taller, but he was still very thin. His finely-chiseled features wore a gaunt, pale look. The brooding, lonely years since his father's death had etched an unsmiling and wistful cast to his countenance.

"Let me show you around," Anderson offered. "I could use a good worker."

There were six chairs, Dan noted. In addition to the main room, the shop had separate rooms where travelers could come at all hours and take warm baths.

Dan agreed to take the job. "First," he said, "I must find a place to stay."

"Move in with us," Anderson said readily. "You'll like my children." When Dan told him about Sally he offered to take her in as well.

A few weeks later Dan and Sally moved into the big two-story house with the Anderson family. What a family it was!

Anderson's wife, Ellen, had lovable ways and spoke in a delightful Irish brogue. She had come to America with one of the waves of Irish immigrants who worked and helped to build the nation.

The oldest son, George, was near Dan's age. Traviata was five years younger than Dan. The family called her Vytie, but Dan called her Viata. Tessie, the youngest girl, was frail and sickly.

Alfred, called Alfie, had been crippled since birth and walked with a limp.

They all greeted Dan and Sally with open hearts. When they discovered that Dan could sing, their love for him doubled. Anderson had taught the children to play musical instruments and Ellen had taught them to sing. Someone in the household seemed to be singing, whistling, or playing an instrument from morning till night. The Andersons reminded Dan of the way his family enjoyed life back in Hollidaysburg.

Dan Williams joined the song-filled, laughter-light Anderson household and began a new life. In the barbershop he became Anderson's chief assistant. Their customers were among the town's most influential citizens, so within a short time Dan and Sally became part of the life of the town. The women of Janesville were delighted to know that Sally made the curls, switches, and hair jewelry that were then in vogue.

Harry Anderson gave Dan a bit of advice that citizens usually offered newcomers: "You can find yourself in Janesville!"

Dan found this to be true. Locked always in a secret crevice of his heart he kept the memory of his father's favorite saying, "We colored people must cultivate the mind." When fall came he enrolled in the Jefferson High School and worked in the barbershop afternoons and evenings. Anderson allowed him to adjust his hours and treated him as a member of the family.

One day something happened to bring the two even closer together. In addition to the barbershop, Anderson also owned the town's biggest band. After work one night Dan went to the band room, picked up a guitar, and began plucking the strings. Soon he was lost in music.

Anderson heard him and came running. "You never told me you could *play* music," he said excitedly.

Dan blushed. He told Anderson about his uncle who had also been a barber and a musician. "I only play by ear," he explained. "I can't read the notes and. . . ."

Anderson stopped him. "I'll teach you. So will Vytie." He walked over and picked up a double bass. "You can start with this."

Within a short time Dan was playing with Anderson's twenty-piece string band. All the other members of the band were white except Anderson and his son, George. The group played for dances and concerts in Janesville and traveled to other Wisconsin towns as well.

Dan's days were so filled with school, music and barbering that he lost the melancholy mood he had brought to Janesville. Even when Sally whispered that she was going to marry the young man who had been courting her, he did not feel unhappy. Sally married and moved to Portage, Wisconsin, and Dan stayed on with his new family.

They were looking forward to an exciting event. Ellen Anderson was expecting another baby any day. On the night the baby came it was Dan who saddled a horse and galloped away to summon a doctor.

The baby was a sturdy boy, and the family named him for Dan and asked Dan to be the boy's godfather. He christened the child. Little Daniel Herbert Anderson added another measure of happiness to Dan's new life.

Daniel Hale Williams had found himself in Janesville.

CHAPTER 4

Cultivating the Mind

The barbershop was quiet. Dan always used the lull between customers for studying. He picked up a history textbook and settled comfortably in one of the barber chairs.

At the sound of footsteps he jumped up and greeted a distinguished-looking gentleman who walked through the door. "Good morning, Mr. Guernsey."

"Good morning, young man. I am glad to see that you like to read." Orrin Guernsey owned a large insurance company. He hung his tall hat on a hat rack and sat in the chair where Dan worked.

"What sort of books do you like to read?" he asked Dan.

"History," Dan said. "I especially enjoy biography."

"I have always been a great reader myself," Guernsey mused. "One day I hope to see a large library here in our town."

The two were quiet for a time. Dan tucked a towel under his customer's chin and began working with the precision he had learned from his father and Harry Anderson. He shaped Orrin Guernsey's beard, styled his jaunty mustache, and trimmed his hair.

After Dan finished, Guernsey looked at him intently. "How would you like to read some of the books from my personal library?"

"I would like that very much, Mr. Guernsey," Dan said. "I have read most of the books in the reading room at the Young Men's Association."

"Fine," said the insurance executive. "Stop by the house and pick out the ones you want."

Dan went the next day. After that, whenever he and Guernsey met, the two would exchange ideas about the books they had read. As Dan read more widely, his mental horizon expanded. New plans and ideas crowded out the old.

Guernsey seemed to guess his thoughts "What about your future, Dan?" he asked one day.

Dan smiled. "I would like very much to go to college."

Orrin Guernsey nodded. "Good decision, lad. If you are thinking of college, you need to study at the Academy. Professor Haire will prepare students for the entrance examinations." He promised to talk to the headmaster.

Guernsey kept his word and Professor Haire agreed to accept Dan as a student. Harry Anderson encouraged this action. "You know I think of you as my son," he said to Dan.

The Janesville Classical Academy occupied the second floor of a downtown building. The structure was far from elegant, but the program was rich and full of cultural experiences.

Dan's first day went well. Professor John Haire had a warm welcome for the serious new student. The second day was a different story.

The father of one of the other students stormed into Professor Haire's office. Word had reached him that Dan was in attendance at the school. "Is that true?" he fumed.

The headmaster spoke politely. "If you mean Daniel Williams, sir, it is. He is a very good student."

"Don't you know he's got Negro blood in him?" The father pounded on the desk, demanding that Dan be removed from the school. Otherwise, he threatened to take his daughter home.

Professor Haire calmly opened his desk drawer. "Here is your daughter's tuition, sir."

The irate father took his daughter home, and the headmaster went on with his work of training young minds. All the other students cheered him for his action. Minerva Guernsey, the daughter of Dan's friend, had her say. "Professor Haire," she cried, "If you put Dan out of school, I'll—I'll leave too."

The principal reaffirmed his decision. "We have no intention of dismissing Mr. Williams from our school."

The incident made Dan more determined to excel in his studies. He took advantage of all the cultural programs that the Academy and the town offered. One evening each week Professor Haire held Literary Round Tables or Home Forums. In these discussion groups the students, along with the townspeople, shared views on wide-ranging topics.

Another citizen planned literary programs of a different kind. Reverend Jenkin Lloyd Jones, a Welshman, organized a Mutual Improvement Club. Every week he gathered the young folk together for reading and discussion in literature, science, current events, and any other topic that might enrich their minds.

The club became so popular that the minister added another feature. A social hour followed the intellectual studies. Dan, Harry, and George Anderson played as a trio for the dancing.

Dan's schoolmates marveled at the change in his personality during these gay social events. Most times he was shy and reserved. When there was music and dancing, however, the gay side of his nature came to the fore.

At the first parties Dan would play the double bass and watch the dancing. Then one night Minerva Guernsey pulled him away from the trio and made him dance.

Harry Anderson joined in the fun. He stomped his foot and made his fiddle sing as he called out a dance pattern.

Swing her high, swing her low,
Don't step on her pretty little toe,
Swing the girl behind you . . .

41

As Dan swung Minerva around, she giggled. "You're the best dancer on the floor," she teased.

Another student watched for a chance to pull Dan away from his bass viol. Ida Williams was his schoolmate at the Academy. She and her stepsister, Carrie Jacobs, were members of one of Janesville's best-known families.

Ida found her chance—not once, but twice. As she and Dan moved across the floor, Minerva whispered a secret some of Ida's best friends shared. "Ida has a great crush on Dan."

After that night it became a game to see which girl could steal Dan away from his instrument. Ida Williams usually won the most dances.

In addition to the local forums and clubs, the town leaders brought in outside lecturers for evening programs. These traveling lecturers provided a popular form of entertainment and education in the 1800s.

The night the famous Robert Ingersoll came to speak, Dan and Traviata sat near the front of the hall. The powerful orator was also well known as a lawyer, politician and writer.

Although his phrases were more poetic, Robert Ingersoll gave the same philosophy Dan's father gave him early in life. "Read!" Ingersoll thundered. "When people read, they begin to reason. When they reason, they progress."

Dan continued to read and progress. His days

43

were so packed with working and learning that one flowed swiftly into another. Suddenly it was spring of 1877, and the day for graduation from the Classical Academy.

The time had come for Dan to make definite decisions about a future career. As much as Harry Anderson needed Dan's help in the barbershop, he never once tried to persuade him to spend his life in that profession. He gave the same counsel voiced by hundreds of black parents in the decades following emancipation. "The young folk of the race must go on to things that were closed to us."

Dan weighed the options before him. His brother Price offered one. "Come and study law with me," Price invited. He had married a Mexican girl and had set up his law practice in Philadelphia. "We could work together as law partners," Price wrote to Dan.

Dan took his brother's advice, but decided to study law in Janesville. One of the town's busy attorneys agreed to let him "read" law in his office. Most students began the study of law by working with a lawyer—another form of apprenticeship.

Dan took care of the clerical work in the lawyer's office. As part of his training he read the law books and began to learn about landmark legal cases. After a few months he discovered that he did not like law any more than he liked shoemaking. Much of a lawyer's work dealt with disputes, one side

44

against another. Dan never had the heart for any kind of bickering. Law was not for him.

He returned to barbering and playing music with the band. He knew that one day he would discover the career that satisfied his inner drives. He waited. And all the while he kept on cultivating his mind.

CHAPTER 5

Doctor's Apprentice

Janesville's popular newspaper was called the *Gazette*. On a late afternoon in 1878, Dan spread out the latest copy of the *Gazette* and began reading. He was alone in the barbershop so he gave his full attention to the news articles.

The longest article flashed the name of Dr. Henry Palmer. The doctor was a familiar subject for headlines. His medical cases made dramatic reading and gossip. This time, the article reported, Dr. Palmer was struggling against great odds to save a patient's life.

Dan sat up straight in the chair, caught up in the drama of the report. The patient had been shot several times. One bullet had passed clean through his body. Another bullet was lodged somewhere in his body, perhaps in a vital organ.

What would happen next? The *Gazette* promised readers a full account in the next issue.

"Struggling to save a patient's life. . . ." The words struck a chord in Dan's memory. He put the newspaper aside and gazed beyond the barbershop, out where the sunset tinted the western hills. The article triggered the memory of information he had learned from one of Professor Haire's books.

It concerned barbering and doctoring.

In earlier years, Dan recalled, barbers had also doubled as doctors. Barbers were called upon to pull teeth and to perform minor surgery, usually amputations. The barber-surgeons were often the ones who supervised bloodletting, the process of drawing blood from the body to treat disease.

Other thoughts surged to the surface of Dan's mind. The symbol of the barber's profession, the red and white pole, was a reminder of the barber-doctor ties. The stripes symbolized the bandages in which barber-surgeons wrapped their patients after bloodletting.

Barber-surgeons. Sitting there in the barbershop, Dan found the answer to his questing. It seemed so simple, so clear to him. This was *it.*

A doctor! He would become a doctor.

Once he had made up his mind, there was no stopping him. He began making plans that very day. As with law, the customary way to begin a career in medicine was through an apprenticeship. The student began learning under a practicing physician who served as his teacher, or preceptor.

Dr. Henry Palmer was considered the best physician in Wisconsin. Dan knew him well. A few weeks earlier he had played with Anderson's band for Dr. Palmer's silver wedding anniversary party.

The next day found Dan at the doctor's red brick home. His eagerness gave him boldness. "I have decided to become a doctor, sir," he announced.

"Will you permit me the honor of studying with you?"

The gray-haired, distinguished doctor looked at the serious young man a long time before answering. He did not give a ready reply. Instead, he fired a barrage of questions.

"Do you know what it means to be a doctor?" he asked. "Do you know what it really means? Would you be willing to leave your warm home and ride through winter storms when patients need you?"

Dr. Palmer then spoke slowly and gently. "Are you able to look upon suffering? Can you face defeat, when you've done all you know how to do? Can you accept death?"

The doctor patted Dan's shoulder. "Go home and think about these things, young man. Medicine is a noble profession, but a trying one."

Dan went home, but he had done all the thinking he needed to do. The more he considered a medical career, the more certain he was of his decision.

In the spring of 1878, he began his medical apprenticeship. For the first few weeks he served as a general helper to Dr. Palmer. He kept the office clean and took care of the medical accounts. In the meantime, he began a methodical program of reading in the field of medicine. Many times over he gave thanks to Professor Haire for insisting that his students master Latin and German. These languages helped him to understand the medical terms he met in his reading. "I keep a dictionary close at hand," he confessed to Traviata. Dan stayed on with the Anderson family and gave a hand in the barbershop whenever he could.

Many times when Dr. Palmer had patients in out-of-the-way places, he took Dan as his driver. His black buggy was a familiar sight on the roadside, with Dan guiding the thoroughbred horses with a long whip. During these long drives Dan learned more about the doctor who was now his teacher.

Henry Palmer had been educated in New York State. He moved to Janesville as a young doctor at a time when thousands of Americans were migrating from eastern states in search of opportunities in the West. When the Civil War broke out, he volunteered as a surgeon and served on the staff of General Ulysses S. Grant. Soon Dr. Palmer was supervising the largest military hospital of the war.

A hospital was one thing Janesville lacked. Medical treatment, including amputations, had to be restricted to the homes. While Dr. Palmer set broken bones or amputated crushed limbs, Dan would hold down the patients. Anesthesia and pain-killers were still rare in many places.

These accident cases kept Dan and Dr. Palmer busy. The new railroads, hunting, unfamiliar farm machinery, all resulted in daily calls from accident victims. Each day for Dan brought a new sense of excitement, for there was so much to learn. Soon he was mixing drugs, wrapping bandages, and even performing simple tests.

After a few months, two new apprentices joined Dan in training. Frank Pember was a year younger than Dan and James Mills a few years older. A close friendship developed between Dan and the other students, and they talked at length about what they would do when they became doctors.

Before they became doctors, they had to attend medical school. The day was passing, Dr. Palmer explained to them, when anyone could go straight from apprenticeship to office practice. Doctors were now expected to spend an additional two or three years of study in a good medical school.

Their preceptor also told the students that they could expect to be ready for medical school in the fall of 1880. Mills and Pember made plans to attend the school of Dr. Palmer's choice. He had sent his son, Will Palmer, to Chicago Medical College, one of the best training centers in the nation. He wanted his three students to go there also.

With his usual daring, Dan planned to join his two friends. He did not know where the money would come from, but his planning never wavered. He had a small savings account, money made from barbering and playing in the band. This would not be enough to buy clothes to take with him, not to mention fees.

Two new inventions reached Janesville and gave him a chance to make extra money. In 1875 Alexander Graham Bell invented the telephone, and in 1879 Thomas Edison worked out his successful principle for the electric light. Always resourceful, Dan helped string the wires for telephones and install lighting along the main street.

This added to his savings, but not enough. He needed money for transportation, school fees, room and board. . . .

Dan wrote two letters. A long, pleading letter went to his mother. Could she send some money? His mother had inherited stocks and property from Grandmother Price, who died four years earlier. She could sell some of these and help him, Dan suggested. After he became a doctor he would be able to support her and his sisters as well.

The second letter was short and businesslike. It went to Mrs. John Jones, a well-to-do widow who lived in Chicago. Her husband had worked with his father in the Equal Rights League. Would she accept him as a boarder? Dan inquired.

The reply from Mrs. Jones came first. "Come and see me when you arrive in Chicago," she wrote. "I will see what I can do for you."

The letter from his mother brought no hope of help at all. She had not been able to manage her mother's inheritance any better than she had managed her husband's. She would try to help later, she promised.

Give up? Never. Not Dan Williams.

He turned to the one person who had never failed him. Harry Anderson solved the problem. "We will borrow some money from the bank," he suggested. "I will sign and be responsible for the payment. I own property and my credit is good." This was no sooner said than done.

After that, the entire Anderson family shared in the adventure of getting Dan ready to go to college. Traviata helped him list all the things he needed to take. George and Harry Anderson went with him to pick out a new suit. Ellen washed and ironed his shirts to perfection. Alfie, Tessie, and Bertie showed their love by tagging behind him wherever he walked.

The day before Dan left for Chicago, Harry Anderson made him sit in the barber chair where he usually worked. With infinite care he fashioned Dan's recently-grown full mustache in the latest style, as befitted an aspiring doctor.

Dressed in his new cutaway suit, and sporting this jaunty mustache, Daniel Hale Williams left Janesville in 1880. He left as a pioneer, as surely a pioneer as other adventurers who had set out with determination to open up the West.

No other black person was blazing the trail that led to the study of medicine at Chicago Medical College.

CHAPTER 6

Medical Student

Dan Williams arrived in Chicago on a golden autumn day. His two apprentice-friends, Frank Pember and James Mills, traveled on the train with him.

The first place they wanted to see was the medical college. They boarded a horse-drawn streetcar and found their way to the campus. Classes were not yet in session, but a friendly janitor offered to show them around.

Each door their janitor-guide opened revealed an exciting arena in which they would study. The eager students walked through the laboratories where they would perform experiments. They studied the skeletons and models, and examined the jars of chemicals and drugs. In awe they sat in the amphitheater where students would come for lectures and demonstrations.

There was one door the janitor refused to open. "That's the dead house," he whispered. This was the room, he explained, that housed the cadavers, the dead bodies that students used for dissection. Dr. Palmer had prepared his students so well that this information only heightened Dan's eagerness to begin classes.

From the medical college Dan walked three tree-shaded blocks until he found the address of Mrs. John Jones. He stood for a moment admiring the large house that held its own with the nearby mansions. Then, taking a deep breath, he sounded the knocker at the door.

"You look exactly like your father!" With these words Mary Jones ushered Dan into her parlor. At once he noted the brocade draperies and expensive furniture. Mrs. Jones' manner matched the elegance of the room.

"Tell me all about yourself," she invited as they sat together on a fine upholstered sofa.

For the next hour the two became acquainted. Dan told about his life in Janesville, his studies, and his work with Dr. Palmer. In a pause in the conversation he looked up at a framed portrait hanging above the fireplace. "Is that Mr. Jones?" he asked.

"Yes, that is a good likeness." Mrs. Jones spoke with pride about her late husband. "He was a quiet man, but a powerful person. One day I hope to see that portrait hanging in the Chicago Historical Society."

Inspired, she launched into a long story about Dan's father's friend. "I was a young bride when my husband brought me from North Carolina to Chicago in 1845. We arrived carrying our precious freedom papers, a watch, and three dollars and forty cents. . . ."

54

Dan interrupted her. "How did your husband build his chain of tailor shops?"

"He was a shrewd businessman," she said. She related how her husband pawned his watch and started a small tailor shop in one room. He learned how to read and write, saved his money, and later opened a chain of shops. The money he made was invested in real estate, and as Chicago grew, he made a fortune.

Mrs. Jones swept her arms in a circle. "This was all underdeveloped land when we bought here. Then the city and the millionaires moved all around us." She leaned closer and whispered. "Our home was once a main station on the Underground Railroad."

Dan listened attentively, part of his mind fascinated by the history. The other part tried to get up enough nerve to broach the subject he came to discuss. Finally he blurted the question. "Would you accept me as a boarder?"

Mrs. Jones smiled. "The roots of our families are deep. It is now up to the members of your generation to carry on the work begun by these great men. . . ."

Dan waited in suspense for her next words.

"I like your manners, young Dan. I can tell that you have good breeding. You may join my family here."

The last barrier between Dan and medical school had been scaled.

He thought it best not to tell his hostess that he came as a penniless boarder. His new braid-bound cutaway and soft silk cravat gave him the air of a man of wealth. He guessed that Mrs. Jones assumed that his father's properties had kept his family comfortably fixed. The fierce Williams-Price pride kept him from baring the truth. Later would be time enough for that, he thought.

Mrs. Jones introduced the others in her family. Her daughter, Lavinia Lee, and her adopted daughter, Sarah Petit, both lived at home. Then there was Lavinia's nine-year-old daughter, Theodora Lee. She and her poodle provided the only loud noise in the house.

Once again Dan became part of a new family. His first letter to Harry Anderson crackled with news about it. "I have a nice room, a bathtub, gas, heat, and first class board," he wrote. "I am faring better and with cheaper board than anyone in Chicago." In a second letter he confessed, "I did not dare to tell her I was so poor. . . ."

One of the best things about his new home was its nearness to the college. Dan walked the short blocks to join Pember and Mills on the day school opened. They sat together in the huge amphitheater as Dr. Nathan Smith Davis, the Dean of Chicago Medical College, addressed the new students.

Phrases from the opening lecture hung in Dan's mind and found a permanent place in his memory. He knew he would never forget them. "Be worthy

of your choice. . . . You must be noble of hearts.
. . . Be ready for hardships. . . . Your rewards will
be priceless and intangible—the satisfaction of
serving mankind.''

Dean Davis made one point clear. Months of
hard work lay ahead of the students who hoped to
become physicians. Dan was prepared for this. His
courses for the first year included anatomy,
chemistry, physiology, and histology. Each required long hours of study. The professors were
notable doctors and set high standards in dress,
behavior and scholarship.

In his weekly letters to the Anderson family Dan
told about his studies and how much he admired his
professors. His letters also relieved his Janesville
family of one of their fears. "I face no racial
hatred," he assured them. He was the lone black
student in the school. Pember and Mills remained
his good friends. In fact, he told the Andersons, his
room was a favorite spot for some of the students to
meet and study. Many students were forced to live
in poor quarters, with inferior lighting and little
heat.

The big problem for Dan was lack of money. His
books and fees took all that he had brought with
him. A part-time job was out of the question since
he needed the time for study. He still could not
bring himself to tell the full truth to Mrs. Jones. He
feared her rejection. Mrs. Jones was very conscious
of status. She had accepted him as her social equal.

If she found out that he was poor, asking for handouts, she might look down upon him. She might even ask him to find another place.

The money worries cast a gloom over an otherwise exciting year. He had no social life, for that would cost money. This did not bother him. "I don't go anywhere but from the house to the college," he said in one of his letters to Janesville. His mother and sisters wrote to him frequently, but they could not send money. One Sunday Dan sat in his upstairs room too worried to study. Would he have to drop out of school? So much depended upon his graduation. If he, a black student, could complete his training, this would pave the way for other students of his race to enroll.

Dan reached for a piece of lined paper and poured out his thoughts to Harry Anderson. Somehow, pride never stood between him and the man who had taken the place of his father.

"I could quit and work for a time," he wrote. He was afraid, he went on, that he might never be given the chance again.

Anderson's reply was prompt. "Stay in school," he urged. With the letter he sent money for Dan's board and a little extra for spending change.

Dan was so overcome with relief and gratitude, his eyes filled with tears. He wrote a reply that same day. "I thank you for your fatherly interest in doing so much for me, as you would for your own children." He knew that the barber had high expenses for his own large family.

The foggy days of fall gave way to winter's numbing chill. Chicago prepared for the holiday season. "When Christmas comes," Dan hinted in one letter, "I should like to come home."

Anderson took the hint and sent money for his fare. The happy days with his adopted family gave Dan the rest he needed from the relentless grind of studying. Once again he could work in the barbershop, play with the band, and join in duets with Traviata.

Dan returned to college and somehow Anderson managed to send the money each month—even though it usually came late. Worries of another kind haunted Dan and the other students that spring, however. A smallpox epidemic broke out. The pest houses were filled to overflowing with the sick and dying. The smallpox vaccination had been developed by Dr. Edward Jenner, but its use was not enforced.

In the midst of the epidemic Dan fell ill. His fever soared above one hundred degrees. "I am a little anxious about my condition," he wrote to Anderson. He was also worried because it was time for final examinations.

Dan sent for his chemistry professor, the famous Dr. Marcus Hatfield. Dr. Hatfield had taken a special liking to the student who asked so many questions.

"It looks like smallpox," Dr. Hatfield diagnosed, "but tests might prove otherwise."

Tests proved that Dan's case was varioloid, an illness with symptoms similar to smallpox. The sickness left Dan weak and despondent. For a long time his hands shook when he tried to write. It took every ounce of will power for him to study and complete his examinations. He passed, but his grades had suffered. He had to settle for a so-so average.

Dan was disappointed. He had hoped to excel in his first year. When he found out that nearly a fifth of his classmates had failed outright, he did feel somewhat better.

"I am tired," he wrote to Traviata.

Her concern came through in her next letter. "Come home, Dan. Come home and rest."

He went back to Janesville. He returned to Dr. Palmer's tonics and to Ellen's cooking. He returned to music with Traviata and with Anderson's band. And he returned to the familiarity of barbering.

These proved to be the therapy he needed. His coloring improved. The ugly marks left by the disease began to disappear from his handsome face.

Dan went back to Chicago and began another year of medical training. Courses were more difficult the second term, but Dan kept pace with the class. By the middle of the year they were doing clinical work. The South Side Dispensary was a clinic run by Chicago Medical College. Mercy

Hospital, one of the largest medical facilities in the city, stood beside the school. The college professors served on the hospital staff, and students went there to get practical instruction.

To Dan, the intensive work was a challenge. His chief worry was lack of funds to pay his school bills. In one of his letters Dan confessed, "I have had only ten cents in my pocket for weeks." In another letter, after Anderson sent the money, Dan poured out his thanks. "You are the only true friend I have," he wrote.

Traviata did not have money to send, but if her encouragement could help Dan get through college, he would get through. In early spring she surprised him with a visit, coming like a shaft of sunlight on a foggy day. Traviata had grown into a stunningly beautiful girl, with warm, endearing ways. She brought along one of her best friends, an Indian girl from Wisconsin. Dan proudly showed off the two beauties to his schoolmates and introduced Traviata as his dear sister.

That week his letter to Anderson dwelled on details of the visit. "Viata made quite a hit," he let her father know. "She had every attention shown her."

The visit cheered Dan and put him in a good mood to study for his second term examinations. This time his grades were much higher than those of his first term. He knew he was a better student. In one of his letters he boasted, "I am twice the man I was a year ago."

"What will you do for the summer?" Traviata asked, hoping to have him home.

"I have volunteered to give some extra hours of work at Mercy Hospital," he wrote.

All summer long, his letters to Janesville were full of news about his work at the hospital. "Frank Pember and I have attended childbirth cases," he told Anderson. "Sometimes we work all night long." Dan and the other students worked throughout the hot summer free of charge. They were glad to get the added experience. Before the end of the summer Dan could write, "I have chances to do operative surgery every week. . . ." These operations were minor ones, but he was learning to use surgical equipment.

To meet his expenses for the summer, he made an arrangement with Mrs. Jones to care for her horses and her buggy. When he had the time, he also served as her driver. In return, she gave him free room and board for the summer. By now she knew his plight.

During the last term help came from his brother. Price had established his law practice on a firm footing. Despite having a wife and several children to support, he promised to send Dan money every month. For the first time since he entered school Dan's worry about expenses ceased. He could turn his full attention to his studies.

A number of new doctors had joined the medical teaching staff. Some were among the greatest scientists in the world. Dr. Christian Fenger from Denmark brought advanced theories from the great clinics of Europe. Of all his teachers, Dan admired Dr. Fenger most.

As Dan worked with the doctors in the clinic and in Mercy Hospital, he could see the old theories and practices beginning to give way to the new. In no area was this more evident than in surgery. Dan's fascination with the study of anatomy naturally led him to an interest in surgery. Fortunately, he was chosen to do practice work on the surgical wards of Mercy Hospital.

It was an exciting time to be studying medicine, especially surgery. By the late 1890s new medical theories were changing the treatment of diseases. Dr. Joseph Lister, the English physician, had proven his theory of antiseptic surgery. Before this, nearly fifty percent of all surgical patients died from infection that set in after surgery. For this reason, patients feared any kind of operation, even the simplest kind.

Joseph Lister proved that this infection was due to germs. If everything connected with the operation could be kept germ-free, he taught, the problem of infection could be greatly reduced. This rule of antiseptic surgery revolutionized surgical procedures.

Other discoveries made surgery easier. Dr. Lister also introduced the use of catgut ligatures for sewing up wounds. Also, the improvement of anesthesia had helped to eliminate the pain and shock of operations. The possibilities for the future were limitless.

Dan thought of this and buckled down to study for the final examination. Part of it was a written test. That would be easy. The months of study in laboratories, wards, and textbooks gave him confidence.

The great test would be the oral questioning. When his turn came, Dan faced the panel of doctors with composure. He hid what nervousness he felt beneath an air of calm confidence.

One after another, the distinguished panel members questioned his fitness to become a doctor. They fired volley after volley of questions to test his understanding of medicine. The heart, lungs, arteries, glands, nervous system, bones, muscles—the doctors tested his knowledge of every part of the human body.

Dan returned their fire; volley for volley, answers for questions. When it was over, he knew that victory was his. He had passed. He could feel it, even before the announcement was made.

He prepared for graduation.

In March, 1883, the medical students assembled in the Grand Opera House in downtown Chicago for graduation ceremonies. The three dozen future doctors marched behind their professors and took the front seats.

Dan was among them. He had grown a full beard for the occasion, the same type of beard once worn by his father. He looked more like the elder Dan than ever.

"Daniel Hale Williams."

The name echoed in the Opera House and Dan walked across the stage to receive his diploma. His great dream was realized. He was now Daniel Hale Williams, M.D.—Doctor of Medicine.

Like medical students before and after him, he repeated the oath of Hippocrates, the ethical code as set forth by the Greek physician to guide doctors in the practice of medicine.

". . . I solemnly pledge myself to consecrate my life to the service of humanity. . . ."

Dr. Daniel Hale Williams, at age twenty-seven, was ready to practice the art of healing.

CHAPTER 7

Doctor Dan

A tall, nattily dressed doctor hurried along Chicago's Michigan Avenue. His right hand swung a medical satchel while his left hand balanced several books. The rhythm of his strides was so swift that he seemed to be almost running.

"Nice morning, Doctor Dan." An old man walking his dog tipped his hat in greeting.

"Hi, Dr. Dan." A young girl on her way to school waved as she skipped along.

Dr. Daniel Hale Williams had a wave, a smile, and a nod for neighbors and patients. It was nearly nine o'clock in the morning and time to open his office. He had rented office space on Michigan Avenue, one of Chicago's main streets. The neighborhood surrounding his office was solid and friendly, with black and white families living quietly as neighbors. He drew patients from both races.

Several patients were already waiting for him that morning. From the day he opened his office he had a sizeable clientele. Mrs. John Jones saw to that. She convinced her friends and fellow church members that they should visit the new doctor, and delighted in telling them that he was like her own son. When she talked about how smart he was, she would say, "Dan sits on more brains than other men have in their heads."

Some of her friends who had known Dan as a student could not bring themselves to call him Dr. Williams. They began calling him "Dr. Dan" as a term of affection. Other patients adopted the name.

These patients talked about their young doctor while they sat in his waiting room.

"He is sincere. He really listens to our problems."

"I like his gentleness. He's the pleasantest person you'll ever want to meet."

"He never charges too much. He grew up poor and understands when people don't have money to pay."

Of course the women liked his looks. "He is so handsome!" they said. "You never see him when he is not immaculate from head to toe."

Dr. Dan set his office hours to suit the convenience of his patients. In addition to the morning hours, he opened the office from three-thirty until five in the afternoon, and again from seven to eight at night. In between these office hours he made calls to patients who were too sick to leave their homes. This made a taxing schedule, but not an unusual one for a doctor in those days.

Dr. Dan made no hospital visits. Beginning doctors seldom had the privilege of joining a hospital staff. Most hospitals had a small staff of

doctors, and positions went to older, well-established physicians.

Dr. Dan faced his first home surgery a few months after he began his practice. One day a well-dressed young lady entered his office.

"Good evening, Julia," he greeted her. "What can I do for you?" He knew Julia LeBeau well. Many Sundays he had listened to the music as she played the organ and directed the choir in Mrs. Jones' church.

"I came to you about my mother," Julia LeBeau told the doctor. "She is in great pain, and I am quite worried."

It was late that night when he stopped at their house. He examined Julia's mother, then took her hand in his. "You have a serious case of hemorrhoids," he told her gently. "An operation will fix you up like new."

"You're not thinking of putting me in the hospital, are you?" Mrs. LeBeau's voice was shrill with apprehension. "I won't consider it. Going to the hospital is the same as going to the grave."

Dr. Dan had grown accustomed to this attitude. He understood the reason behind it. Many people considered hospitals to be in the same class as poorhouses, jails, and insane asylums. Hospitals were often gloomy places. Since most sick people entered hospitals only after they became critically ill, the death rate was high. This strengthened the impression that one did not go to the hospital to get well, but to die.

Dr. Dan soothed his patient. "Don't worry, Mrs. LeBeau. I will perform the operation in your home." He turned to Julia. "Sunday will be the most suitable day." He explained to her that Sunday was the day many doctors performed home surgery, since they did not have the heavy shedule of office hours.

Dr. Dan stood up and looked around the house. "The dining room will be the best area," he said, beginning his plans. "The large table will provide a solid operating surface."

Early Sunday morning he was back to give more directions. "The curtains will have to come down," he said. "Julia, you can help me scrub the walls and floors of the dining room."

Mrs. LeBeau bristled with indignation. "My home is spotless, I'll have you know. There is no need for scrubbing and dusting."

With patience Dr. Dan explained aesthetic cleanliness and antiseptic cleanliness. A surface might appear to be clean, when in reality there may be millions of disease-causing microbes lurking there.

Dr. Dan and Julia scrubbed every inch of the room, then sprayed everything with carbolic acid. A big pot on the kitchen stove bubbled where his surgical instruments were being sterilized. A kitchen pan was made antiseptic to hold the instruments. The big dining table was draped with germ-free sheets.

Dr. Dan was a strict disciple of the teachings of Dr. Joseph Lister. There must be no risk of bacteria getting in the wound to cause infection.

The extra hours of surgical duties at Mercy Hospital had given Dr. Dan unusual confidence for a beginning doctor. The years of using barbering tools had given his hands and fingers a dexterity he transferred to the surgical instruments.

He had been sure and swift as a barber, and he was sure and swift as a surgeon. In the quiet of the dining room he removed the offending hemor-rhoids. He stayed with the patient for the remainder of the day to be sure that her progress went well.

Thanks to his painstaking work to kill germs, there was no infection during the post-operative days. Mrs. LeBeau recovered and sang the praises of her surgeon throughout her church. "That young doctor is something else!"

During the months that followed, Dr. Dan performed many such operations on dining room or kitchen tables. Each operation made him more determined to perfect his surgical skills. The big drawback was the lack of operating room facilities and up-to-date equipment.

A remedy for this came in 1884. One of his teachers recommended his appointment as a demonstrating doctor on the staff of the South Side Dispensary, the clinic run by Chicago Medical

College. For a black doctor this was quite a pioneering feat. As part of his duties Dr. Dan demonstrated surgical techniques for medical students and gave them instruction in anatomy.

Much to his surprise, Dr. Dan liked teaching. He was not a forceful, dynamic lecturer, but his voice was clear and well pitched for public speaking. The years as a part-time vocalist with Anderson's orchestra had improved his diction. Students would hold him after class to tell him how much his lectures helped them to understand anatomy.

One of the students taught by Dr. Dan was a young man from Minnesota named Charles Horace Mayo. None of them could realize that this eager student would one day team up with his brother to form the world-famous Mayo Clinic in their hometown of Rochester, Minnesota.

Dr. Dan kept in close contact with his former professors as well as with schoolmates. Another of his professors was so impressed by his work that he recommended Dr. Dan for the position of assistant physician at the Protestant Orphan Asylum. All who knew Dr. Dan realized how dearly he loved children. This was a job without pay, but one that brought considerable experience, prestige, and publicity. Dr. Dan had the publicity he needed when all 250 children in the orphanage came down with measles at the same time!

An even more prestigious appointment came to Dr. Dan in 1889. The Governor of Illinois appointed him to fill a vacancy on the Illinois State Board of Health. This marked the first time that a black doctor had become a member of the Health Board.

These were years when diseases such as small-pox, scarlet fever, and typhoid hit cities in waves of epidemics. As the lone black member of the Board, Dr. Dan pushed to enforce stricter rules and health standards. He recommended enforcement of rules for vaccination so that people, especially children, would be immunized against highly infectious diseases. He also helped to press the city of Chicago for better plumbing and sewage disposal.

After these appointments, Dr. Dan's name frequently appeared in the newspapers. Invitations to dinner and parties came to him weekly. "What a catch Dr. Dan would make for some lucky girl," mothers whispered.

Most times Dan was too busy to do more than send a polite regret. Once in a while, though, he would appear late at a party, after his visiting hours were over.

"Dan's here!" someone would call out.

"Did you bring your guitar?" someone else would ask.

The host would find a guitar. Soon everyone in the room would be swaying and singing as the doctor's agile fingers moved up and down the strings.

He had many friends, but he had not singled out

73

any special girl for attention. Mrs. Jones urged him to look around. "I always hoped you would marry Traviata," she told him one day.

"Marry Viata?" Dr. Dan shook his head. "Oh, no. I could never marry her. She is like my sister."

He visited his Janesville family whenever he could. He began paying Harry Anderson the money for his schooling as soon as he started working. When the Anderson family faced a series of tragedies, Dr. Dan traveled back and forth to Janesville to be with them.

Dear, gentle Tessie, who had always been frail, died at the age of seventeen. A few months after her death, Ellen Anderson died suddenly from a mysterious illness. Realizing how despondent Harry Anderson was, Dr. Dan suggested to him that he move his family to Chicago. Dan wanted Traviata to study music under a famous teacher.

Anderson took his advice and moved the family into an apartment in Chicago. Dan saw to it that Traviata began studying under the world-famous organist, Clarence Eddy. It was known that Eddy accepted only the most talented students.

At the same time George Anderson decided that he wanted to be a dentist. He began his studies at Chicago College of Dental Surgery at the age of thirty-seven. Dan felt good that he could help his adopted family and repay them for some of their kindness to him.

By many friends, Dr. Dan was considered a great

success. He was too much like his father, however, to be satisfied with his progress. There were still too many black people in need of help. As injustices and repressions increased in the South, black Americans crowded to large cities of the North and West. They came with high hopes, looking for opportunities. They often found unemployment, overcrowded conditions, and poverty.

"Where will my people get jobs?" Dr. Dan wondered. Equally important, he wondered where they would get health care.

Dr. Dan searched for answers. One of his frequent remarks was, "To solve the medical problem, we must solve the race problem."

CHAPTER 8

America's First Interracial Hospital

Dr. Dan rode out to check on two patients who had undergone surgery in their homes. Both were doing quite well. Neither case had developed infection.

By the time he left the last patient, a fierce December snowstorm began swirling over the city. Streets were already slippery with an icy-white coating. The air was so cold that Dr. Dan's breath frosted on his reddish-brown mustache.

There was still another stop to be made. He had promised to visit the home of Reverend Louis Reynolds, pastor of the African Methodist Episcopal Church. He guided his thoroughbred horse through the snow and headed toward Dearborn Avenue.

Reverend Louis Reynolds greeted the surgeon at the door and led him into a lamplit parlor. "I sent for you because I need your help," Rev. Reynolds began.

"I listen to problems all day long," Dr. Dan replied with a smile. "You are not feeling ill, are you?"

In answer Rev. Reynolds called his sister. "Emma, come and meet Dr. Dan Williams."

An attractive girl came into the parlor. "This is my sister, Emma Reynolds," the minister introduced her. "She came to Chicago hoping to study nursing." He shook his head. "Emma, you tell Dr. Dan the story."

I've wanted to be a nurse ever since I can remember," Emma spoke up. She told Dr. Dan how she had applied to enter the programs that had been opened to train nurses. All had turned her down. "I know I am qualified," she said, her eyes flashing her anger. "The story is always the same. Almost none will accept a black girl as a nursing student."

Dr. Dan gave a deep sigh. He had worried over this matter for years. Many hospitals were now setting up nurse training schools. The advances being made by medicine, especially surgery, meant that nurses would be in demand more than ever in the future. More nurses must be trained in surgical procedures.

Dr. Dan began pacing back and forth in the room, as he usually did when he was in deep thought. "Where can the girls of our race get training?" he asked aloud. "For that matter, where can the young doctors go?"

He turned to the minister, a look of despair on his face. "Even I, who train medical students in surgery, cannot practice what I know in any of the city's hospitals."

Rev. Reynolds agreed. His problem at the

moment, though, was to get immediate help for his sister. "You are a member of the State Board of Health," he said. "Can't you use your influence and get Emma into one of the programs for training nurses? You know a lot of people."

Dr. Dan started pacing again. Suddenly he whirled around. "No. I don't think I'll try to get Miss Reynolds into a training course. We'll do better. We'll get down to brass tacks."

His voice softened, the way the strings of his guitar mellowed when he played a love ballad. "We'll start a hospital of our own, and we'll train dozens and dozens of nurses."

His voice swelled louder as he unfolded a secret dream. "Doctors could come to this hospital for internship. Nurses could come for training. Patients could come and leave with a new attitude toward hospitals. This hospital will. . . ."

The minister stopped him. "The idea is good. But where will we get the thousands of dollars needed to get a hospital started?"

"That's what I mean by getting down to brass tacks," Dr. Dan retorted. "Let's start planning tonight."

So the planning for a new hospital started that night in a lamplit parlor. The plans buzzed in Dr. Dan's head as he braved the blustery snowstorm to reach home. He was like his father when he had a crusade to lead. And this was a crusade worth leading.

Over the next weeks he moved over Chicago faster than a windstorm moving across the lakes. He was the general, laying out the campaign plans. The campaign was to build a hospital.

He organized his good friends of both races to be his captains. And mighty good captains they proved to be.

Traviata, excited by the idea, worked as hard as Dr. Dan. She had become a superb musician and often accompanied noted singers in concerts. Traviata had also become a bride. She married Dr. Charles Bentley, a dentist.

Dr. Dan and captains such as Traviata rallied the preachers. The preachers used their churches as meeting places. Dr. Dan went from church to church, talking about the project.

"This hospital must be a project for all citizens," Dr. Dan insisted from the beginning. "All races must work to build it. All races will be served by it."

These speeches satisfied a doubt spoken by some people. A hospital built by black people would be a step backward, they thought. It would perpetuate segregation in medical care.

"This will be a hospital for Negroes," he told audiences, "but it will not be a Negro hospital. It must be an institution of interracial good will, dedicated to medical service and the training of Negro interns, technicians, and nurses—all the nurses we can train."

His enthusiasm was contagious. Chicago's millionaires began donating large sums of money. Businessmen joined the fund-raising and urged their employees to do likewise. The names of donors read like a Who's Who of the Chicago business world.

Marshall Field, the great merchant, was head of the largest wholesale and retail dry goods establishment in the world. Philip D. Armour, the industrialist, had introduced refrigeration and developed the giant Armour & Co. meatpacking firm. George M. Pullman, the inventor, had designed the Pullman sleeping cars for trains.

These businessmen, along with others, gave funds and encouragement for the project. One of the first wealthy men to donate money was the famed newspaper publisher, Herman Kohlsaat. His newspaper, the *Inter Ocean,* gave publicity and brought in more benefactors.

Captains and committees vied with one another to see which one could raise the most money. The weekly rallies, bazaars, chicken suppers, dances, fish fries, and other socials brought the people together in a venture like nothing before. Children were not left out. Sunday schools collected pennies and nickels for their contributions. Everyone in the city should be a part of the historic undertaking, Dr. Dan encouraged.

As the money continued to come in, Dr. Dan and a committee looked around for a building. They found a three-story building with space for at least twelve beds.

Dr. Dan suggested the formation of the Provident Hospital Association. This was a stroke of genius. Everyone who gave a donation became a member of the Hospital Association. This meant that hundreds of people in Chicago could consider themselves as playing an important part in getting the hospital started.

The new Provident Hospital and Training School Association was incorporated in January, 1891.

Squads of men volunteered to scrub and paint the old building to spruce it up for the grand opening. Groups of women workers began cooking and sewing and planning the opening ceremonies.

The doors of Provident Hospital officially opened on May 4, 1891. Committees outdid themselves in planning the Grand Opening Benefit Party. Excited crowds jammed the sidewalks and filled the halls. "Everybody who was anybody came," one newspaper reported. Gaily decorated booths, representing all nationalities, sold food and souvenirs. Streamers and flags carried out the international theme of the occasion.

Guests came bearing gifts—money, beds, food, medicines, supplies, books. Dr. Dan moved quietly through the throngs, thanking the guests for making the hospital possible. "In time we will work for a new, more modern building," he promised.

The building was makeshift, and lacked the

up-to-date equipment of the larger hospitals. The staff was superb, however. Provident's doctors included some of the best-known names in medicine. Dr. Dan's colleagues gave their services free of charge. Dr. Christian Fenger, his former teacher, was among them.

Dr. Dan searched for qualified physicians from his own race. Traviata's husband, Dr. Charles Bentley, had served for three years in the Dispensary of Rush Medical College. He joined Provident as the oral surgeon. Dr. Allen Wesley had been a professor at Fisk University before he became a distinguished physician. He was put in charge of gynecology, the treatment of women's diseases.

Dr. Austin Curtis, a recent graduate of Chicago Medical College, won the honor of becoming the first intern. Seven young girls, including Emma Reynolds, made up the first nurse training class. Hundreds of other girls had asked for the chance.

One serious problem in staffing arose. Dr. George Cleveland Hall, a practicing physician in Chicago, applied to join the staff. Unfortunately, his medical degree had been obtained from a school that was not certified.

Dr. Hall was black. He was also a popular political figure in the community. Despite this, Dr. Dan rejected the application. "Only qualified doctors will be permitted on the staff of Provident," he had announced. When it came to high medical standards, he was unyielding.

Other members of Provident's Board of Directors disagreed. They finally persuaded Dr. Dan to add Dr. Hall to the staff.

Dr. Hall was a proud man. He considered the incident a slight to his reputation and blamed Dr. Dan. "I will not forget, and I will not forgive," he vowed. The seed was sown for a feud that would last for years to come.

Dr. Dan was too busy to pay attention to Dr. Hall's anger. He had to keep Provident going. A severe depression had hit the country. Most of the patients who came were poor and unable to pay the full fees. Dr. Dan had to keep his crusade and his captains working long after the hospital opened.

"Pledge to give something to the hospital every month," he urged. "If you live in the country, ask the farmers for eggs, butter, and vegetables of all kinds. Search your homes for good linens, and old rags." He always added another reminder. "You can speak a good word for the hospital when you are among strangers. And you can pray for it."

Prayers, hard work, and gifts kept the hospital open. Housewives who baked bread made a few extra loaves for the patients. Those who canned fruits and vegetables remembered to put some aside for Dr. Dan's hospital. One street peddler stopped by every afternoon and donated all the fruits and vegetables he had not sold. Nursing students talked among themselves of how Dr. Dan would reach into his pocket and give the cook his own money to buy food for the patients to eat.

At least a third of the patients were white—mainly Germans, Swedes, and Irish.

The relentless work and public speaking took a toll. "Dr. Dan looks old and tired," his friends worried. They urged him to slow down.

Dr. Dan's answer was to enroll in advanced courses at Chicago Medical College, which had recently merged with Northwestern University as its medical school. The university was a short distance from Provident. This meant that Dr. Dan could easily affiliate with the school, and the medical students could come to the hospital and observe him perform surgery.

The historic year of 1893 brought the great World's Fair to Chicago.

Dr. Dan's cousin, Frederick Douglass, was serving as the United States Minister to Haiti. Douglass came to the Fair as one of the main speakers. Still handsome and erect at seventy-six, the statesman stirred the crowds with his thundering oration.

Afterward he went on to speak at a large church. The audience filled the collection plates as a gift to Douglass. He, in turn, brought the money as a gift to Provident.

Dr. Dan, wearing his white hospital coat, ran to the sidewalk to meet Douglass and escorted him from the carriage. A loud cheer went up from the crowds standing along the sidewalk to watch. The cheering kept up as the two men walked arm in arm into the new hospital.

The visit of Frederick Douglass gave a big boost of publicity that Provident needed.

At the end of the first two years of operation the hospital had admitted over two hundred surgical cases. Many of them came because of Dr. Dan's growing reputation as a surgeon.

America's first truly interracial hospital was in business to stay.

CHAPTER 9

"Sewed Up His Heart!"

July 9, 1893, was hot and humid in Chicago. The scorching heat wave wrapped the city like a sweltering blanket and blistered the sidewalks. Rising temperatures sent thermometers zooming toward one hundred degrees.

The heat and high humidity took a heavy toll on young and old, animals and people. Horses pulling carts and streetcars dropped in their tracks. People fainted from heat prostration and sun strokes. No relief was in sight.

Doctors and hospitals were kept busy. The new Provident Hospital was no exception. Dr. Dan kept close watch on his patients. Making his rounds, he looked as immaculate as always, despite the heat. After his late-afternoon rounds were over, he retired to the closet-like room he used for his office.

Suddenly, a young student nurse burst into the room, her long starched skirt rustling as she ran.

"Dr. Dan!" she gasped. "An emergency! We need you."

Without a word Dr. Dan dropped the report he was reading and hurried to the room set aside for emergency cases. The lone hospital intern, Dr. Elmer Barr, came running to assist.

The emergency case was a young man. He had been brought in by his friend, who gave sketchy information. The patient's name: James Cornish. His age: twenty-four years. His occupation: laborer. The illness: he had been stabbed in the chest.

The frightened friend tried to explain what happened. James Cornish had stopped in a neighboring saloon on his way home from work. The heat and a few drinks caused an argument among the customers. A fight broke out. When it ended, Cornish lay on the floor, a knife wound in his chest.

"How long was the knife blade?" Dr. Dan asked as he began his examination. This would give a clue to the depth and seriousness of the wound.

The victim had not seen the knife blade. Nor had his friend. Action in the fight had been too fast and furious.

Dr. Dan discoverd that the knife had made an inch-long wound in the chest, just to the left of the breastbone. There was very little external bleeding. Nevertheless, Cornish seemed extremely weak, and his rapid pulse gave cause for concern. The X ray had not yet been invented, so there was no way to determine what was happening inside the chest.

Dr. Dan knew from experience that such cases could develop serious complications. James Cornish must be kept in the hospital, he decided. And he must be watched closely.

That night Dr. Dan slept in the hospital. He did

this often when there were serious cases. As he had feared, Cornish's condition worsened during the night. He groaned as severe chest pains stabbed the region above his heart. His breathing became labored. A high pitched cough wracked his sturdy frame. The dark face on the pillow was bathed in perspiration.

Dr. Dan watched the wounded man carefully all night. The next morning, as he took the patient's pulse, he voiced his concern to the intern. "One of the chief blood vessels seems to be damaged," he said to Dr. Barr. The knife must have gone in deep enough to cut the internal mammary artery, he explained. The heart itself might be damaged.

James Cornish showed symptoms of lapsing into shock.

Both doctors knew that something had to be done, and done quickly. Otherwise Cornish would surely die within a matter of hours.

But what?

The only way to know the damage done would be to open the chest and look inside. In 1893, doctors considered this highly impracticable. For surgery, the chest was still off limits.

Standing beside the patient's bed, the barber-turned-doctor faced the situation squarely. Later he would recall how he weighed the risks of that moment. Thoughts tumbled through his mind as furiously as flurries in a wintry Chicago snowstorm.

He knew that medical experts repeatedly warned

against opening the thorax, the segment of the body containing the heart and lung. Heart wounds were usually considered fatal. As a medical student, Dr. Dan had read a quote from an eminent physician-writer. "Any surgeon who would attempt to suture a wound of the heart," the surgeon wrote, "is not worthy of the serious consideration of his colleagues."

So far, doctors had followed this cautious advice.

The risks were there for him and for Cornish. If he did not attempt an operation, Dr. Dan reasoned, the patient would die. Nobody would blame the doctor. Such cases often died.

On the other hand, if he opened the chest and Cornish died anyway, there would be certain condemnation from medical groups. His reputation as a surgeon would be questioned, perhaps lost.

The odds were against both him and Cornish. But Daniel Hale Williams had never allowed the odds to intimidate him.

Dr. Dan lifted his chin, the way he did when he faced a challenge. The storm of doubts suddenly swept away, leaving his mind clear and calm as a rain-washed April morning.

The surgeon quietly told his decision to the intern. Two words he spoke. "I'll operate."

The word spread quickly through Provident hospital. Like a small army alerted to do battle, student nurses rushed to get the operating room ready and prepare the patient. They knew Dr.

Dan's strict rules regarding asepsis, or preventing infection. The instruments, the room, furniture; everything that came in contact with the patient must be free of microbes that might cause infection.

Meanwhile, Dr. Dan sent a hurried message to a few doctors who often came to watch him operate. The intern, a medical student, and four doctors appeared. Dr. George Hall of Provident's staff was there. So was Dr. Dan's friend, Dr. William Morgan. The circle of watchers gathered in the operating room; four white, two black.

Dr. Dan scrubbed his hands and arms thoroughly. Then, with a nod toward his colleagues, he walked over and looked down at Cornish, now under the effects of anesthesia. Strong shafts of sunlight slanted through a window, giving the doctor's curly red hair a glossy luster. His thin, sensitive mouth drew taut with concentration.

The surgical nurse, proud of her training, stood at attention.

Scalpel!

A loud sigh escaped one of the doctors when the light, straight knife touched Cornish's bare skin. After that there was silence from the onlookers.

None of them knew what would happen next. How would the body react when air suddenly hit the chest cavity? Would vital chest organs shift too far out of place? Dr. Dan could not benefit from the experiences of other doctors. No paper had been

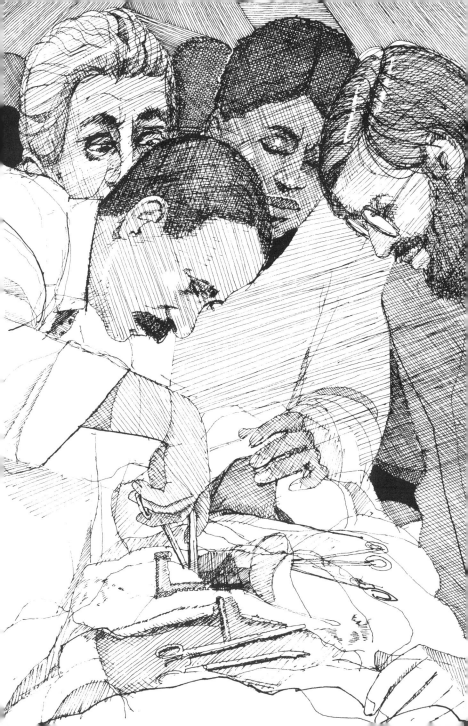

written, no lectures given to guide him. Dr. Dan was pioneering in an unexplored territory. He was on his own.

The surgeon worked swiftly. He had to. The surgeon of 1893 did not have a variety of anesthetics or artificial airways to keep the patient's windpipe open. Blood transfusion techniques were unknown. Penicillin and other infection-fighting drugs had not been discovered.

Quickly, Dr. Dan made the incision, lengthening the stab wound to the right. Expertly, he cut through the skin and the layers of fat beneath it. Now he could see the breastbone and the ribs. He made another cut to separate the rib cartilage from the sternum.

Long years of studying and teaching human anatomy gave his every movement confidence. Working with precision, he made his way through the network of cartilages, nerves, blood vessels. A few inches from the breastbone he cut through the cartilage to make a little opening, like a trapdoor.

Bending his head close to the patient's chest, he peered through the opening he had made. Now he could examine the internal blood vessels.

Now he could see the heart!

The tough bundle of muscles throbbed and jerked and pulsated, sending food and oxygen through the body. Dr. Dan examined the pericardium, the fibrous sac that protected the pear-shaped heart and allowed it to beat without rubbing against other parts of the body.

At each step, Dr. Dan reported his findings to the group of observers. The vital pericardium was cut—a tear of about an inch and a quarter in length. He probed further. Yes, there was another puncture wound, he reported, about one-half an inch to the right of the coronary artery. Had the knife moved a fraction of an inch, Cornish would have bled to death before he reached the hospital. Also—Dr. Dan paused—the left mammary artery was damaged.

As the problems were ticked off, the atmosphere in the room grew more tense. The temperature rose above one hundred degrees. Yet not one doctor reached to wipe the perspiration that poured down hands and faces. No one took note of the time. It seemed as though the moment were somehow suspended in history, awaiting results.

Dr. Dan kept on talking and working. The small wound in the heart itself should be left undisturbed, he advised. It was slight. The tear in the pericardium was a different matter. That had to be repaired.

Now the surgeon's hands moved with a rhythm born of knowledge, practice, and instinct. Strong hands; flexible enough to pluck tunes from guitars and violins. Sure hands; steady enough to string high telephone wires. Quick hands; made nimble from years of cutting hair and trimming beards and mustaches.

These hands now raced against time to save a life. Dr. Dan tied off the injured mammary artery to prevent bleeding.

Forceps!

Now he had to try and sew up the heart's protective covering. Meticulously, he irrigated the pericardial wound with a salt solution of one hundred degrees Fahrenheit. There must be no chance of infection after the chest was closed.

Using the smooth forceps, he held together the ragged edges of the wound. Against his fingers the fist-sized heart fluttered and thumped like a frightened bird fighting to fly free.

Sutures!

Despite the rapid heartbeats, the master surgeon managed to sew up the torn edges of the pericardium. For this he used a thin catgut. After that he closed the opening he had made, again using fine catgut.

Another kind of suture would be used for the skin and cartilages, he informed the circle of watchers. He changed to silkworm gut, using long continuous sutures. This allowed for quick entry if infection or hemorrhage developed later. Over the outer sutures he applied a dry dressing.

The operation was over. James Cornish was still alive.

Dr. Dan straightened his aching back. Only then did he stop to wipe the perspiration from his face.

Like figures in a fairy tale suddenly brought to life by magic, the circle of doctors began to move and talk. They rushed to congratulate the surgeon. "Never," said one, "have I seen a surgeon work so swiftly, or with so much confidence."

Each of them dashed from Provident to spread the news. Daniel Hale Williams had opened a man's chest, repaired the pericardium, closed the chest; and the patient's heart was still beating.

How long would Cornish live? Worried watchers waited in suspense. Had the doctor repaired the heart but killed the patient?

During the hours that followed the operation, Dr. Dan scarcely left Cornish's side. Alarming symptoms developed, and he made careful notes. The patient's body temperature rose to 103 degrees. His pulse raced at 134 beats a minute. Heart sounds became muffled and distant. Seizures of coughing shook his frame.

Dr. Dan shared his fears with Dr. Barr. Fluid had collected in the pleural cavity. This meant another operation.

He waited a few more days to give Cornish more time to gain strength. Three weeks after the first operation, Cornish was again rolled into the operating room. As before, Dr. Dan made an incision, this time between the seventh and eighth ribs. Through this opening he drew five pints of bloody serum.

Thanks to his careful adherence to antiseptic surgical techniques, there was no infection, and there were no further serious complications. Fifty-one days after James Cornish entered Provident with little chance of living, he was dismissed—a well man.

A news reporter from Chicago's *Inter Ocean* newspaper came to Provident to interview the surgeon and get the story first-hand. He found Dr. Dan more anxious to talk about his interracial hospital and the program for training nurses than to talk about the historic operation. The reporter had to coax details from him.

Nevertheless, the reporter's story came out with an eye-catching headline: "SEWED UP HIS HEART!" Another heading read: "DR. WILLIAMS PERFORMS AN ASTONISHING FEAT. . . ."

The *Medical Record* of New York later carried Dr. Dan's own scientific account of the techniques and procedures he had used during the operation. His case created world-wide attention, for it was the first recorded attempt to suture the pericardium of the human heart.

His pioneering operation gave courage to other doctors to challenge death when faced with chest wounds. Dr. Dan's techniques were copied by other surgeons, step by step.

The phrase "Sewed Up His Heart" became closely associated with the name of Daniel Hale Williams. The historic operation on James Cornish helped to advance the progress toward modern heart surgery.

CHAPTER 10

"Freedmen's Needs You"

"There will be big changes in Washington under this new administration. Mark my word."

Judge Walter Q. Gresham spoke to Dr. Dan from firsthand experience. He had been appointed Secretary of State by the new President, Grover Cleveland.

Judge Gresham and Dr. Dan sat talking in the Judge's Chicago home. The two had been friends for several years. Judge Gresham was one of the first white men to give money for the new Provident Hospital.

As they talked, the Secretary added a new twist to their conversation. "I want to talk with you about a serious matter," he began. "President Cleveland plans to make improvements at Freedmen's Hospital. The surgeon-in-chief will be replaced. I would like to recommend you for this position."

Dr. Dan's face showed his surprise. "My place is here—at Provident. The hospital needs me. . . ."

His friend stopped him. "You have the hospital well organized. The staff is strong. Other doctors can carry out your plans."

The two men debated the idea for another hour.

They reviewed the story behind Freedmen's Hospital.

The story began during the Civil War. Thousands of former slaves began flocking to Washington, D.C., looking for a place to stay. Homeless and penniless, they took shelter in whatever spot they could find. These crowded quarters added to the health problems of the freedmen. The children fared worse. Three times as many black children were dying as were white children.

To handle the emergency, the government authorized the Freedmen's Bureau to establish an emergency hospital.

Freedmen's Hospital, Asylum and Refugee Camp was set up in an old army camp in the nation's capital. Later, a permanent location was found on the grounds of Howard University. The University had been started by the United States government and named for General Oliver Otis Howard, head of the Freedmen's Bureau.

During the thirty years that followed, Freedmen's had been neglected by government officials. It was run more as an asylum than as a hospital. Freedmen's had never developed into the medical center it should have been. Now Dr. Dan was being invited to take on the challenge.

It was a sobering thought. Secretary Gresham reached out a hand toward Dr. Dan. "If it is service to your race you're thinking of," he said, "Freedmen's needs you more than Provident."

Once again, Daniel Hale Williams faced a crossroads in his career. Provident, or Freedmen's? Chicago, or Washington, D.C.?

Freedmen's and Washington won. Dr. Dan submitted an application for the position as surgeon-in-chief, the highest administrative job at the hospital. It offered the top administrative post open to a black doctor anywhere.

Doctors from all sections of the country, black and white, wanted the job. It carried considerable prestige. Each sent an application and letters of recommendation.

Dr. Dan's letters of recommendation came from his teachers and colleagues. All had high praise for his personal and professional qualities. One of them wrote, "I know him to be a man of honor and as a member of society, a superior gentleman. Professionally he stands at the top of the medical profession."

Dr. Dan won the appointment.

Then the unexpected happened. A group of friends persuaded Dr. Dan to go for one last weekend of quail hunting in southern Illinois. While hunting, Dr. Dan was accidentally shot in his right foot.

By the time his friends rushed him to Provident, inflammation of the veins of his leg had developed. Doctors treated him and ordered that he stay in bed.

Dr. Dan left his bed too soon. There was too

much to be done before leaving Chicago. This brought on a relapse. The infection spread, and the lymph glands became involved.

His doctors were now alarmed. Finally they gave their dreaded diagnosis. "Your leg should be amputated. The infection is endangering your life."

"No!" Dr. Dan was adamant. "Send for Christian Fenger," he ordered.

His old teacher and friend knew all about treating gunshot wounds. His experience in treating soldiers during the Prussian wars in Europe had made him an expert. Dr. Fenger operated on his former pupil's leg, but did not amputate. For more than six months he tended Dr. Dan, fighting to save his life as well as his leg.

"I will never forget these months when I faced becoming a cripple," Dr. Dan said many times. He would never, he vowed, amputate an arm or a leg if he could possibly save the life otherwise.

While he lay ill, rumblings came from Washington. "Why is the new surgeon-in-chief so long in coming? One newspaper article questioned Dr. Dan's fitness. "Has a sick man been chosen to head Freedmen's? He is a fitter subject for a hospital than for the management of one."

It was a sad period for the sick doctor. While he fought for his own life, Traviata became ill. He could not go to her. He was crushed when her husband brought him news of her illness. She had tuberculosis. The same disease that had taken his father now threatened to rob him of his adopted sister.

He finally recovered enough to leave Chicago for Washington in September, 1894. Friends who saw him worried that he looked so thin and frail.

Frail or not, he looked distinguished as he stood to meet the staff of Freedmen's Hospital. Dr. Dan had shaved his heavy beard and now wore only his silky, drooping mustache. His illness and the years of establishing Provident had left a pensive look on his face and given a deep-set, penetrating gaze to his eyes.

Dr. Dan was introduced by the president of Howard University, Reverend Jeremiah Eames Rankin. He knew the white minister as a longtime fighter for the equality of black people and as a hymn writer. Dr. Rankin had written the familiar hymn, "God Be With You Till We Meet Again."

Although he was still weak, Dr. Dan lost no time in unpacking and starting his new job. He was given the apartment in the medical building so that he could be readily at hand.

Conditions were far worse than he had imagined. The five wooden buildings that were built as emergency barracks thirty years before were still in use. These were the hospital wards. The offices and the operating room were in the one brick building. This meant that after surgery the patients had to be taken on stretchers from the brick building out to their beds. At mealtimes, all the patients who could walk made the trip from the barracks to the main building where the kitchen and dining room were located. All the patients, regardless of the nature of their ailments, were thrown together in a helter-skelter fashion.

The funds allotted for the hospital were far too low to run a medical center. There were no nurses. Medicine was administered by a "ward mammy" who called out the hours when patients were to take their own doses. And patients who were well enough helped with the work. Dr. Dan read one recent hospital report that boasted of this. "The following articles have been made by the women: pillow cases, 140; sheets, 162; towels, 103; aprons, 154; nightgowns, 60. . . ."

The death rate was high. The hospital staff did not have full control over which patients were admitted, or when they were discharged. This was controlled by the Department of the Interior, the government agency that administered the hospital. Many patients were considered wards of the government, since they had no place to go.

"My people deserve better," Dr. Dan said sadly. It took him less than a month to reorganize. Seven essential departments were set up: medicine, surgery, dermatology, respiratory and bronchial, gynecology, obstetrics, and genito-urinary. In addition to these, Dr. Dan established pathology and bacteriology services.

The hospital staff was too small. Drawing upon

his successful methods used at Provident, Dr. Dan invited noted doctors of all races to come to Freedmen's as consultants and serve for no fee.

The Freedmen's Nursing School opened to provide trained nurses. Dr. Dan sent to Chicago for Nurse Sarah Ebersole, an expert in surgical nursing. She was made superintendent of the new nursing school.

Announcements went out to newspapers, schools, and churches, inviting young women to apply. Five hundred applicants asked to join the new nursing program. Only thirty-seven could be taken. These students worked twelve hours a day, twelve months a year, with two vacation weeks. They received five dollars a month for spending money and their caps and books free.

"Freedmen's must serve as a national training center for Negro doctors and nurses," Dr. Dan announced.

He took special pride in the student nurses. The standards he set for them were high, but no higher than those he set for himself. Their starched skirts and big white aprons must be immaculate at all times, they were told. Nurses were never to be seen around the hospital grounds without wearing their caps.

Dr. Dan called each of them "daughter." Standing beside a seriously ill patient, he would look to the nursing student, his piercing eyes intent. "Daughter," he would say, "this patient must live."

And the student nurse, catching his zeal for healing, would answer, "Yes, Dr. Dan. The patient will live."

Freedmen's became a changed place. Order replaced chaos. Cleanliness and beauty brightened the old wards. Dr. Dan insisted that roses or blooming plants be grown in the gardens as long as weather permitted. Every day, bowls of cut flowers were placed in the dining room and on the wards for patients to enjoy.

One of the most frustrating problems Dr. Dan faced was the prejudice people held against Freedmen's. It was considered a hospital for only the very poor.

Dr. Dan started a new and bold program at Freedmen's to help change this attitude. He began holding open house in surgery. Every Sunday afternoon the public could sit in the amphitheater and observe Dr. Dan or fellow surgeons operate on patients. The faces or bodies of the patients were never revealed fully, but the spectators could see the methods used by the surgeons.

Naturally, Dr. Dan was criticized by many people for such an advanced step. Some objected to his holding the open house on Sundays. Some even went so far as to say Dr. Dan held the demonstrations to publicize his own skills.

Nevertheless, the demonstrations did bring people into the hospital. Many liked what they saw.

105

It was a new Freedmen's. Dr. Dan had accomplished his main objective.

Another frustration for Dr. Dan was the lack of a medical group with which he could affiliate. He missed the contact with Dr. Fenger and his associates in Chicago. The local medical group in Washington refused to accept black doctors.

Dr. Dan had a remedy for this too. He joined with a number of doctors to form an interracial medical group, the Medico-Chirurgical Society of the District of Columbia. The members met to exchange ideas and to discuss common medical problems.

A few months later, Dr. Dan helped to form a national medical organization. A group of black physicians from all over the country met in Atlanta, Georgia and organized the National Negro Medical Association.

The founding members wanted Dr. Dan to be the first president, but he declined. He did agree to serve as vice-president.

Despite the mammoth task at Freedmen's, Dr. Dan enjoyed living in Washington. He bought a house there for his mother and his two youngest sisters. He managed to have dinner with them at least once each week. Florence, with his financial help, was now studying to become a teacher. Alice was already a gifted seamstress.

There was another home he visited often. Cedar Hill, the estate of Frederick Douglass, became a favorite place to sit and talk. Dr. Dan would drive in his carriage to Anacostia and chat with Douglass about some of the problems he encountered at Freedmen's.

Douglass, known as the "Sage of Anacostia," had sound advice for his cousin. "There is only one way you can succeed, Dan, and that is to override the obstacles in your way. By the power that is within you, my boy, do what you hope to do."

The pioneering physician took his advice and surmounted the roadblocks in his way.

He continued to revolutionize Freedmen's. During his first year there, the hospital treated more than five hundred surgical cases. Amazingly, only eight of them died. Dr. Dan, modest as he was, had to admit that this was an astounding achievement.

CHAPTER 11

Alice

An atmosphere of suspense and waiting hung over Freedmen's. Workers watched from windows and doorways.

Suddenly a nursing student called out. "It's coming! It's coming!"

Doctors, students, and attendants all rushed toward the front door. A horse-drawn vehicle rounded the corner. A cheer of welcome went up from the hospital staff as they ran to inspect Freedmen's latest prize.

An ambulance!

The ambulance looked somewhat like a covered delivery wagon. On the side of the van-like wagon could be seen in bold letters the name, FREEDMEN'S HOSPITAL. A red cross painted beneath it identified it as a wagon of mercy.

The driver sat on a high seat in front, holding the reins of a beautiful sorrel horse. For the first time, the hospital had a means of transporting patients.

The ambulance did not wait long to be called into action. An urgent message reached Provident from a nearby hospital. A critically ill woman had been brought to them but they had no bed for her. Could Freedmen's send the ambulance to get her?

At Freedmen's the patient was rushed into the receiving room. She was screaming with pain and seemed unable to speak. An emergency call went out for Dr. Dan, who was lecturing in another part of the hospital.

Nursing students fumed as they hurriedly prepared the woman for examination. "I'll bet that hospital could have found a room," one of them said.

"You know they could," the other agreed. "They did not take her because of her color."

Dr. Dan came and took over. He bent over the woman, who was a tiny, dwarf-like person barely four feet tall. With quick, sensitive fingers he examined the patient. Suddenly he straightened up and gave a quick diagnosis. "The patient is about to deliver. She is also having convulsions."

One nursing student gasped in disbelief. The tiny woman showed no signs of advanced pregnancy. But she knew better than to question. If Dr. Dan said it was so, then it was so.

The surgeon-in-chief knew that he faced a crisis situation. In emergencies such as this he always used the case to teach. So, while his hands worked methodically, rhythmically, he lectured to the interns and doctors who watched. "Convulsions at childbirth are often fatal," he told them. He could try to save the mother, he went on, but to save both the mother and baby seemed almost an impossibility. He decided to try for the impossible.

The interns were familiar with the way Dr. Dan's words rapped out in sharp, staccato fashion when he operated under emergency conditions. Yet his voice was never raised. "I will perform a Caesarean section," he announced. It was risky, he explained, but it was his only chance of saving both mother and baby. Delivery through the birth canal would be impossible.

The announcement brought surprised looks, but no comment. The observers stood hushed and tense. All of them knew that this meant cutting through the abdominal wall and removing the baby from the uterus. The technique was named for Julius Caesar, the Roman emperor, because he was supposedly born in this manner.

It was a new method in the United States and, in fact, in most of the world. Until recent years, a Caesarean section had almost always resulted in death.

One of the doctors broke the silence and whispered a question. "Wouldn't it be less of a risk if you only tried to save the mother's life?"

The reply from Dr. Dan came as sharp as his surgical knife. "You always try to save both lives."

Deftly, Dr. Dan made a clean incision in the abdominal wall. He was master of himself and the situation, and all who watched him knew it. Another incision had to be made through the wall of the womb, or uterus, in order to lift the baby out.

When the surgeon lifted the child, alive and

kicking, a smile of admiration crossed the face of each onlooker. "The baby weighs about seven pounds," he told them. "It is perfectly normal." Handing the child to an attendant, he turned his attention to the mother, closing the incisions he had made.

Mother and child lived. Both went home healthy, thanks to the medical care of the changed Freedmen's Hospital.

The surgical case reached the newspapers. "Snatched from the Womb!" one headline read. In their articles the local reporters called attention to the changes and new programs Dr. Dan had brought to Freedmen's. These articles helped to further dispel the prejudices held against Freedmen's by middle-class black families. The result was more patients and harder work for the surgeon-in-chief.

He welcomed the hard work. Tragic events clouded his personal life that unusual year of 1895. In February, Washington and the world mourned the passing of Frederick Douglass. The black race had lost its most forceful spokesman, and Dr. Dan had lost his trusted counselor.

The year also brought the death of Dr. Henry Palmer, the Janesville physician who had started Dr. Dan toward his medical career. That was not the end. Another close friend and adviser, Judge Walter Gresham, also died. It was he who had talked Dr. Dan into coming to Freedmen's.

Then heartbreaking news came from Chicago. Traviata, so full of laughter and music, had died of tuberculosis. Dr. Dan was losing so many of the people he loved and respected.

The most shocking news concerned his brother. Price, so successful, so sophisticated, was also lost to them. Dr. Dan took Price's body to Annapolis and buried him beside his father in St. Anne's Churchyard.

There was one bright gleam of happiness that slipped into Dr. Dan's life to brighten the gloomy days.

Alice.

Her name was Alice Darling Johnson. She was a teacher. Dr. Dan came to know her well when her mother developed cancer. He respected her mother's dread of hospitals and took a team of doctors to perform an operation in the Johnson home. After this, Alice Johnson looked to him as a friend.

One early afternoon the hospital staff saw Dr. Dan, faultlessly dressed, leaving the hospital in his surrey. Beside him rode Dr. William Warfield, an intern whom Dr. Dan had promoted to first surgical assistant. They drove away in the direction of Ninth Street.

When Alice Johnson daintily stepped down from her porch to meet them, passers-by stopped to gape in admiration. Whenever she walked down the streets heads usually turned and stared, so striking was her beauty.

The trio drove to the next block to pick up Alice's best friend, Caroline Parke, called Caddie. Dr. Dan then guided the surrey through the tree-bordered streets and out into the spring-dressed countryside. "We are going on a picture-taking expedition today," he told them. Photography had become a popular pastime in Washington, and the surgeon made it his hobby.

As Alice posed for pictures, Dr. Dan adjusted his camera to catch the exquisite lines of her features. She was tiny—only five feet, four inches—but she appeared taller. Her friend Caddie often said, "Alice is matchlessly formed."

She was. Her oval face was framed by dark hair that curled around her forehead. Her large brown eyes, fringed with long lashes, held a somber, mysterious look.

"Smile, Alice," Caddie urged. "Smile when he snaps your picture." They knew that Alice seldom smiled.

The camera excursion was one of many fun-filled trips for the foursome. They went on picnics, on tours of the Smithsonian Institute, to concerts at Ford's Theater, and to parties. Dr. Dan seldom attended the parties until late, but he would arrive in time to drive Alice and Caddie home.

Some months passed, and friends noticed that Dr. Dan was escorting Alice alone. Each time he saw her he learned more about her family background. He understood why she was so devoted to her ill mother.

"Mother has spent her entire life caring for me," Alice told him. She unfolded the fascinating story, bit by bit.

Isabella Johnson lived as a black servant girl in the home of a rich Jewish merchant. In the Richmond, Virginia home she was treated almost like a member of the family. The merchant's son fell in love with the pretty servant girl, but laws and custom prevented them from marrying.

The son went off to fight in the Civil War, and while he was away, a little girl was born to Isabella, the servant girl. The child was Alice Darling.

"What happened to your father?" Dr. Dan wanted to know.

"I seldom talk about him, Hale," she said. Alice called Dr. Dan by his middle name. Her voice dropped to a whisper as she revealed her father's identity. "His name is Moses Ezekiel."

"Do you mean the world-famous sculptor?"

"Yes. He is my father."

"Do you hear from him?" Dr. Dan asked gently.

Alice touched the gold locket she wore on a chain around her neck. "He sent me this from France." She showed him her Italian brooch, which she often wore pinned to the neck of her dress. "He sent this gift from Italy."

The friendship between Alice and Dr. Dan

deepened with the passing weeks. At the same time, the problems at Freedmen's mounted.

As a government agency, the hospital was subject to political pressures and infighting among officials. In 1897, William McKinley became the twenty-fifth President of the United States. This swept in a new administration.

A congressional committee was appointed to investigate all charitable and reformatory institutions in the District of Columbia. Meanwhile, the Secretary of the Interior, Cornelius Bliss, announced a civil service examination to appoint a new surgeon-in-chief of Freedmen's Hospital. All this was done without a word to Dr. Dan.

He was stunned. Mr. Bliss refused to see him. He finally received an appointment with the senator who headed the investigation committee. He was James McMillan of Michigan.

In the conference, Dr. Dan outlined for the senator the improvements he had made at the hospital, showing statistics to prove his claim. Senator McMillan was so impressed that he contacted the Interior Secretary, and within a short time another announcement was sent out: "There is no vacancy at Freedmen's Hospital."

However, the congressional committee continued the investigation. Dr. Dan was called to testify. One of the accusations was that Freedmen's took too many cases from all parts of the country.

Dr. Dan reminded the lawmakers how few

hospitals there were to care for black people. He had tried, he explaind, to build a national institution. Dr. Dan used his testimony, not to defend his administration, but to educate the lawmakers.

"I would especially like to ask the committee," the surgeon testified, "to examine into my methods and the work of the hospital and from this examination to judge the possibilities of the future."

The investigation saddened the surgeon. He won his case, but there was no joy in the victory. Freedmen's was a political grab-bag, always at the mercy of the changing administrations.

After the investigation, Dr. Dan made two sudden decisions that took his friends by surprise.

The first decision was announced in his letter of resignation from Freedmen's. In it he stated that he had accomplished the work he had set for himself, "to give the patients the benefit of modern methods. . . ."

The second decision was headlined in the April 2, 1898 issue of a local newspaper. Dr. Daniel Hale Williams had married Alice Darling Johnson.

It was a quiet wedding, the article reported, due to the recent death of the bride's mother. The wedding took place at the bride's residence, with only close friends present. The bride wore blue, not white, because of her bereavement. Her best friend, Caroline Parke, played the wedding march.

The marriage ceremony was read by Rev. Jeremiah Rankin, president of Howard University.

The famous poet, Paul Laurence Dunbar, was a close friend to Dr. Dan. Dunbar wrote a light-hearted lyric to honor the occasion.

> Step me now a bridal measure,
> Work give way to love and leisure,
> Hearts be free and hearts be gay—
> Doctor Dan doth wed today.

CHAPTER 12

"Dr. Dan's Back!"

"Dr. Dan's back!"

Friends and patients spread the news and welcomed the popular physician back to Chicago.

A gala wedding reception gave Dr. Dan and his bride an official welcome. One news report presented a vivid picture of the festivities. "Music, dancing and refreshments contributed to the enjoyment of the evening. . . . Melodies from sweet-voiced mandolins emanated from behind a row of palms. Conventional attire was imperative for the men. The gowns worn by the women were elaborate."

The reporters agreed with the guests that the new Mrs. Williams was beautiful. "Mrs. Williams wore a rich white brocade trimmed with pearls and liberty silk. She had diamond ornaments and carried a bouquet of bridal roses."

One of the happiest guests present was a tall, good-looking young man who kept smiling at the groom. Dr. Dan finally pulled himself away from well-wishers and walked over to talk with him.

"It is difficult to think of you as grownup and ready to go to college."

"Thanks to you," his godson answered, "I will be entering Northwestern University in the fall."

The young man was Daniel Herbert Anderson. It was interesting that Harry Anderson had helped to educate Dr. Dan, and the doctor in turn had inspired two of Anderson's sons to choose medical careers.

The morning after the reception found Dr. Dan in his office, working as though he had never been away. He was happy to have an office practice once again.

After office hours he hurried over to Provident Hospital. During his years in Washington he kept in close touch with Provident's directors, and helped to plan the new building that was opened in 1896.

No sooner had Dr. Dan become settled in his office and hospital routines, than troubling news reached him from Washington. The political pot was still boiling over Freedmen's. Dr. Austin Carr, Provident's first intern, was chosen to succeed Dr. Dan as surgeon-in-chief. Meanwhile, a fight developed over which agency should control the hospital.

The Secretary of the Interior ordered another investigation. Several members of Dr. Dan's former staff, anxious to secure their own positions, testified against his administration. Dr. Dan, they intimated, may have used hospital funds to buy instruments for his own use.

One of those who betrayed him was Dr. William Warfield, his friend and the former intern he had trained to be a surgeon. Another was nurse Sarah Ebersole.

Bewildered by the situation, Dr. Dan traveled to Washington and faced another panel of investigators. The panel members seemed determined to prove that he had used hospital funds to buy items that were not used for the patients. The master surgeon who had saved lives, who had developed hospitals, and had performed the first suture of the human heart, was forced to answer petty accusations and questions.

"I see that on April 2, 1897," the panel chairman said as he read old bills, "one Kelly's cystoscope, one calibrator and one Reverdin needle were purchased. Do you remember anything about them?"

"Do you know whether any calibrators were bought for the hospital?"

"Were six tongue depressors bought on July 19, 1897?"

The relentless questioning went on and on, as the panel members sought to force Dr. Dan to admit that he was guilty of mismanagement. And he, speaking as patiently as though he were teaching first-day medical students, tried to teach the panel about medical instruments. He explained that they expected some instruments to be broken or discarded.

Certain types of operations, he told them, required delicate, costly needles. Once damaged, they could never be used again. Forceps were often broken and had to be replaced. It should be expected that over a period of nearly four years many of the items purchased would not be there—especially when five hundred surgical operations were performed every year.

The panel members showed surprise when Dr. Dan itemized the expensive instruments he had bought with his own money. When operating, he told them, he preferred to use the most up-to-date instruments available. Hospital budgets did not always permit the purchase of these.

The exhausting ordeal finally ended. Citizens such as Rev. Jeremiah Rankin testified strongly on Dr. Dan's behalf. Once and for all, his name was cleared.

This was small comfort. He was hurt beyond repair. Some of the persons who had perjured themselves and testified against him were those who had worked closely with him. Dr. Austin Carr had worked shoulder to shoulder with him during the lean years at Provident. They scrubbed operating room walls and performed menial tasks as well as brilliant surgery.

Nurse Ebersole had been a trusted member of his team. Dr. Dan discounted the gossip that buzzed around Washington. Nurse Ebersole had reportedly set her cap for the handsome surgeon-in-chief when she came to Freedmen's. She was disappointed over his marriage and this was her way of striking back at him.

Gentle Dr. Dan had not grown up in the rough-and-tumble world of the streets. He had never learned to fight back. He had learned to bury his hurt in hard work and silence.

He did this now. He returned to Chicago a changed man. "I will never take an assistant into my confidence again," he told Alice. For a long time he refused to have even a secretary. He handled his affairs himself.

This was understandable, but it was unfortunate. There were so many young black doctors who could have worked with him and learned his surgical techniques. He was such a marvelous teacher!

Alice Williams tried to soften his mood with small dinner parties in their home on Forrest Avenue. Typical of these parties was the evening a dozen friends gathered for dinner and music. While they dined, the ladies exclaimed over Alice's hand-painted china.

"She paints them herself," one guest said.

"I know," her companion whispered. "And she's as dainty as the china she paints."

The men had more admiration for the brilliant pheasants mounted on the dining room walls. Dr.

Dan took pride in showing off his handiwork. He had brought them back from one of his hunting trips and, with his surgeon's hands, had stuffed and mounted them. Alice was not allowed to put any other decorations on the walls that might compete with their beauty.

After dinner the guests gathered in the sitting room, which Alice had furnished in a tasteful manner. "Where is your guitar?" a friend called to Dr. Dan.

Alice brought the guitar, and the guests saw a sudden change in the surgeon's personality. He relaxed completely as he led his friends in singing. His fine tenor voice shifted from the ballads to a new waltz tune that had the country singing.

> I love you truly, truly dear,
> Life with its sorrow, life with its tear,
> Fades into joy when I feel you are near,
> For I love you truly, truly dear.

"You know the lady who wrote that song, don't you?" one of the male guests asked his host.

Dr. Dan smiled wistfully. "I surely do. Carrie Jacobs and I knew each other in Janesville. She is Carrie Jacobs Bond now. Her stepsister was one of my dearest friends." Ida Williams was now Mrs. Lord, and a mother. When her son became ill she brought him to Dr. Dan for surgery.

On a night not long after this party Alice

whispered some news that cheered her husband far more than her dinner parties. They were expecting their first child!

Alice was overjoyed. She knew how dearly her husband loved children. Even though he had dozens of godchildren, a baby of his own would make up for some of the sadness of the past years.

Alice put her artistic talents to work and decorated an upstairs bedroom to be used as a nursery. Dan's sister Alice sent samples of her fine needlework in baby clothes, and his patients showered them with gifts for the longed-for heir.

Then all the hopes, the joy, the excitement were dashed the night the baby was born. The child died at birth. Neither Dr. Dan nor all the experts he brought in could save the little life. The doctors had all they could do to save Alice.

Afterward, riding home with some of his doctor-friends, Dr. Dan collapsed and burst into tears. The loss of his child seemed the last straw in the long string of deaths. For a long time after this he became upset whenever anyone gave him a baby to hold.

Alice remained ill for a long, long time. "I went to the very brink of the grave," she wrote to her friend Caddie. "I am still hoping to have another baby," she confided.

Dr. Dan had his work. For him, his work was like recreation. As another way of instructing, he wrote long research papers to explain some of his surgical techniques and medical findings. Some of these papers were read before medical groups. Some were printed in journals. In several instances his views clashed with those of eminent doctors. This was especially true when the topic dealt with diseases believed to be common to black people.

Myths and misconceptions had arisen and had been printed and passed down as truths. These myths were due partly to racial prejudice, and partly to the limited experience which many white doctors had in treating black patients. "These misleading myths must be replaced by scientific data," Dr. Dan said.

In one of his papers he dispelled the notion that the blood of black persons was less pure than that of white patients. "The color of the skin in this country," he reminded, "furnishes no index of the purity of the blood. . . ." He pointed out the many shades of skin coloring in his racial group, from rich ebony to fair mulatto. "Who is to determine," he questioned, "where the line is to be drawn?"

Dr. Dan's work was his life. Alice devoted her time to civic and social projects. She organized kindergarten classes for poor black children. She helped women find jobs to suit their talents. Frequent newspaper articles described Alice's busy social life.

"Mrs. Daniel H. Williams gave a very instructive

talk to the Phillis Wheatley Club on how to teach children of the sewing school. . . ."

"Mrs. D. Williams turned her home over to the King's Daughters for an evening of Shakespeare." Each guest who came gave a donation, which went to various charities.

Alice tried hard to please Dr. Dan and to please his friends. "I am making Hale a pretty good wife," she wrote a friend in Wasington.

So the nineteenth century drew to a close with both Dr. Dan and his wife busy. He was still excited about the art of healing. The rapid progress being made in his profession meant that there was always something new and exciting to learn.

The progress was mind-boggling. Theories of antisepsis were now firmly established. Anesthesia had been improved. Physicians were giving more attention to studying the functions of the brain and nervous sytem in health and disease. This gave rise to a new specialty—neurology.

Best of all, marvelous inventions added to the rapid progress of medical science. Thanks to the work of Dr. Wilhelm Roentgen, the German physicist, doctors would soon be looking at organs inside the human body. Dr. Roentgen had invented the invisible X rays that go through solid substance. Dr. Dan knew that such innovations would revolutionize diagnosis and treatment.

His main concern was still the lack of good medical care for black people. As unemployment rose, and sections of Chicago became ghettos, health problems increased.

What could be done? Dr. Dan worried. He knew that this condition existed in countless other cities. It was time to begin crusading for solutions to this perplexing problem.

CHAPTER 13

Medical Crusader

Dr. Dan placed a period at the last line of a letter and signed his name with a flourish. His stationery was of fine paper and carried his name in bold printing.

The letter was of crucial importance to medicine and to the black race. He addressed it to Booker T. Washington, Tuskegee Institute, Alabama.

He had known the founder of Tuskegee Institute for a long time. The two men were the same age. Each year Dr. Dan sent clothes, books, and money to help students in the struggling Alabama school.

Booker Washington visited Freedmen's while Dr. Dan headed the hospital and later wrote to say how impressed he was by what he saw. He invited the surgeon to come to Tuskegee and set up medical and nurse training departments.

Dr. Dan was now proposing a better plan. Why not build a hospital, he suggested in the letter. "You could draw work from all over the South," Dr. Dan wrote, "and build a Monument there and care for thousands of poor people who die for want of surgical attention." At the close of the letter Dr. Dan offered to come to Alabama and give his services free of charge.

He waited anxiously for an answer. None came. For reasons he never explained, Washington had changed his mind about building a medical facility at that time.

Dr. Dan was disappointed, but he did not give up. The one thing he was willing to fight for was better health care for his race. The dream of building hospitals kept him writing letters and planning.

One day an invitation came from Dr. Robert F. Boyd, on the staff of Meharry Medical College. "Come and visit us," Dr. Boyd invited. The two men knew each other, for Dr. Boyd had been elected as the first president of the National Medical Association. Dr. Dan wrote that he would come.

He knew the history behind Meharry. The medical college had developed from a small school founded to educate ex-slaves.

The medical school was named in honor of the five Meharry brothers who donated money to construct a building. The five brothers told how they had been befriended by black people during their early years, and the gift was a way of showing their appreciation.

When Dr. Dan visited Meharry, the school still lacked hospital training for students. They were refused use of the Nashville hospitals. Their makeshift "hospital" was set up in basement rooms.

Dr. Dan spent several days at Meharry, impressed by the staff and students, and by the possibilities for the school. While there he held a mini-clinic, demonstrating surgical procedures in their basement quarters.

Before he left he talked with members of the staff. "If black doctors are to practice modern medicine," he told them bluntly, "they must be given intern training." Dr. Dan began pacing the floor, clasping and unclasping his hands. He was warming up to an idea. If white hospitals refused to admit black doctors and interns, then the people of Nashville would have to do as the people had done in Chicago.

"We can't sit any longer idly and inanely deploring existing conditions," he told the group. "We must start our own hospitals and training schools."

The staff agreed. "We could gather the people of Nashville," they said, "if you'll just talk to them as you talked to us today."

So it was settled. Dr. Dan returned in January, 1900. True to their word, the doctors had assembled a large crowd at the Phillis Wheatley Club in Nashville. The crusading surgeon spoke to them of his dream for building hospitals.

"We should have a hospital and training school in every city in the South with a population of ten thousand," he preached.

He was inspirational, but he was practical. He offered step-by-step suggestions for setting up a hospital. "Rent a house," he told them. "Choose one with ten or twelve rooms, preferably with a basement. Furnish it simply, so that it can be easily cleaned and kept clean. . . ."

Dr. Dan grew emotional that night when he saw the hundreds of faces looking at him and hanging on every word. He was not unlike the preachers in the Price and Williams families who had swayed audiences in generations before him.

He was candid. He described the discouragements faced at Provident and Freedmen's. "Few enterprises," he warned, "even those for the betterment of mankind, have smooth sailing at the start." He advised the listeners not to be discouraged by criticisms, or expect others to do what they should do. "When we have learned to do well what we have the ability to do, we will have accomplished much toward changing sentiment toward us."

Dr. Dan flashed a winning smile. "Then, when you have completed your preparations, open your doors and success will be assured." As a parting advice he offered them the same counsel Frederick Douglass had given him. "The only way you can succeed is to override the obstacles in your path. By the power that is within you do what you hope to do!"

The packed room cheered him as a king. They did more. They followed his plan of self-help. By the time he returned in September to hold a clinic, they had opened a small hospital. They followed the Provident plan and opened in a large house, first with twelve beds, then later added more. Out of this small beginning would grow one of the finest medical centers in the South.

It was in the small hospital that Dr. Dan held his famous clinics every year. The Williams clinic proved the high point of the school year for Meharry students. Alumni came as well as students. So did doctors from other parts of the country. And in time white doctors began to join them.

As he had done at Provident, Freedmen's and Howard University, Dr. Dan demonstrated the possibilities of modern surgery for saving and improving life. Most of the doctors had never seen such masterful techniques. "They never saw such a clean, swift operator," one doctor remarked. "Why, Dr. Dan could sew up a man faster than any sewing machine ever made."

Every year the surgeon would take the train to Nashville and hold the clinics, featuring "rare and difficult" operations. He gave his service free. And long after he had left, the students and teachers would be discussing the things they had seen.

Many a poor student, working at menial jobs to pay his way, would be encouraged to bear the hardships a little longer and become a doctor. After all, Dr. Williams had been poor. He had worked at odd jobs when he was young. If he could do it, so could other youths. And children still in grade school made up their minds to go to Meharry and become physicians.

Dr. Dan took his philosophy of self-help to other cities in the South. "You must better yourselves," he said again and again. "Build hospitals!" Black people took up the challenge. Hositals and training schools opened in city after city—Dallas, Atlanta, Knoxville, Memphis, Louisville, Birmingham, Kansas City, St. Louis.

Soon requests were pouring in for Dr. Dan's help, far more requests than he could honor. Some requests were for him to lecture. He went whenever he could, but he always had two restrictions. He refused to lecture to any medical group if black doctors were not permitted to sit in the audience. By the same token, he would not operate in a hospital where black patients were not accepted.

When he had the chance to instruct groups, he would caution them about amputating arms and legs. He made dozens of slides to illustrate injuries he had treated. Some cases had seemed hopeless, but he had saved the precious limbs.

One day in 1904 a six-year-old Irish boy was brought to Provident Hospital. He had fallen from a wagon and fractured his ankle. From ankle to knee the tissues were badly lacerated and infected.

Doctors who examined the lad shook their heads

in pity "Poor little fellow," they sympathized. "The leg will have to be taken off."

Dr. Dan shook his head; not in pity, but against such a decision. He never forgot the time he had nearly lost his own legs. "This is a poor boy who must some day make his living," he said. "I'm going to wait until I feel there is no chance to save that leg."

He treated the little boy with the same care Dr. Fenger had given him. The care paid off. The boy was finally able to go home with only a limp to show for the accident. Even the limp, Dr. Dan assured him, would disappear in time.

Whether in a home, a clinic, or a hospital, Dr. Dan seemed happiest when he was healing patients. For twenty-five years now, he had been practicing the art of healing and he never lost his zeal for it. In 1908, doctors and friends from around the country joined to honor his silver anniversary in medicine.

The guests came bearing gifts. The most stunning gift of all was a huge silver bowl engraved with the names of thirty-seven Chicago physicians. One name was missing, that of Dr. George Hall.

The years since the early days of Provident had not softened the harsh feeling that Dr. Hall held for Dr. Dan. When a doctor came to ask him to join in honoring the surgeon, he sneered. "Curse him!" Dr. Hall shouted. "I'll punish him worse than God ever will. I'll see he's forgotten before he's dead."

The threat cast a dark cloud of warning over the lovely celebration. Like the curse of the old witch at the christening of the princess, Dr. Hall's words seemed an omen. Those who knew him well realized that he was only biding his time.

CHAPTER 14

Triumphs and Tragedies

Dr. Daniel Hale Williams stood before the members of the National Medical Association. As usual he was one of the stars of their annual meeting. Each year he came to read papers and to operate.

In his clear, instructive style, he lectured to the doctors before beginning a surgical demonstration. The patient was suffering from a large tumor, he informed the observers. There were many complications. Always the teacher, he gave detailed accounts of the problems and the procedures he would use.

As he began to operate, the crowded amphitheater became silent. Doctors leaned forward, intently watching every move.

Dr. George Hall sat on the front row, his eyes following Dr. Dan's hands. Suddenly he leaned toward the surgeon. "If it's too much for you," he taunted, "why don't you come out and close up?"

The out-of-place remark rang through the gathering like a rifle shot. Dr. Dan immediately stopped lecturing. Without uttering another word he completed the operation, pulled off his rubber gloves, and only then looked at the doctors. "Thank you, gentlemen," he said, and strode from the room.

At another meeting of the NMA, a doctor placed Dr. Dan's name in nomination to be president. Dr. Hall was determined that this would not take place. He waged a fierce behind-the-scenes political battle against the surgeon. "Some people are among us only when honors are being dispersed," he told members.

Dr. Dan's name went down to defeat. He would not have accepted the appointment anyway. He was far too busy. After all, he could have been the first president, had he not declined. Nevertheless, the manner in which he lost hurt him deeply.

The feud between the two doctors spilled over into Provident Hospital. While Dr. Dan was away at Freedmen's, Dr. Hall secured a place on important hospital committees. He was a hard worker, and made himself indispensable to the staff. Finally he was put on the most important committee of all—the committee that hired the staff. Dr. Dan, on the other hand, was content to work with the finance committee.

So it was Dr. Hall now, not Dr. Dan, who was undisputed boss of Provident. He loved the hospital. There was no doubt about that. Provident was as much his life as it was Dr. Dan's. The trouble was, there did not seem to be enough room there for both doctors.

The disagreement went on. Dr. Dan held a

disdainful attitude toward Dr. Hall's ability as a doctor and did not hide the fact. Once, when Dr. Hall was operating on a patient, another doctor had to take over in order to save the person's life. Dr. Hall considered himself a great surgeon. Dr. Dan called him a "butcher."

The vendetta seemed to be building to a climax.

The climax came on the heels of one of Dr. Dan's highest achievements. In 1908 he was invited to become associate attending physician at St. Luke's. This appointment to one of Chicago's largest and richest hospitals brought wide publicity and high praise.

Dr. Hall saw the appointment as an act of disloyalty to Provident and to the black race. Most of St. Luke's patients were white, and rich. "He is selling out the black race," Dr. Hall declared. "If he is serious about better health care for black people why doesn't he spend all of his time at Provident?"

Dr. Dan refused to defend his acceptance of the appointment, or to reply to Dr. Hall's accusations. In an earlier letter to Booker T. Washington he had explained that any reconciliation with Dr. Hall seemed impossible. "Many times I have subserved for peace and harmony," he said, "but it never came."

Dr. Hall made a move that he knew would cut Dr. Dan to the quick. He proposed that Provident's board of directors issue an order to the surgeon. Some board members fought against the order, but

Dr. Hall's influence prevailed. The order was approved.

Dr. Dan read the letter from the board members in absolute disbelief. "You are hereby requested," the board ordered, "henceforth to bring your patients to Provident for treatment."

The request was preposterous. This meant that all of his hospital patients, regardless of circumstances or the nature of their illness, must be brought to Provident for treatment. Incredible!

What could he do?

Dr. Dan calmly assessed the choices opened before him, as though he weighed the options in an emergency surgical situation. He could obey orders and bring all his patients, white and black, to Provident. Or, he could go to the board and ask them to retract the order. His fierce Price-Williams pride discarded this option. Besides, when it came to healing he could never draw a racial line. He had been trained to heal *all* people.

With his lips set in a thin, taut line Dr. Dan pulled a sheaf of paper toward him. In a short, terse letter to the board he resigned from the hospital he had founded.

Part of Dr. Hall's vow had come true. He had punished Dr. Dan in a way he knew would crush him.

Dr. Dan refused to discuss his reasons for resigning. Many people did not understand why he had left Provident. Others who understood urged him to fight back. "Speak out and let everyone know what Dr. Hall is doing," they advised him.

In reply he would set his jaw at a stubborn angle. "If the people don't know me yet," he said, "they never will."

In private he explained his views to Alice. "It would seem undignified," he said, "to engage in a public squabble with Dr. Hall." Nothing she nor anyone else could say would change his decision.

Unfortunately, many black people took his silence to mean a change of his interest in what happened to them. Perhaps he had grown so famous that he no longer wanted to be identified with his own race, they said.

Had he been of a different temperament, Dr. Dan could easily have made his position clear. He could have explained that the work at St. Luke's gave him the opportunity to work with expensive equipment that he would not find in the other hospitals. Dr. Dan was already serving in other hospitals of the city, but Dr. Hall had not objected to these appointments.

Equally important, if Dr. Dan was successful in the assignment, more and more doctors of his race were sure to receive appointments to the staff of St. Luke's and other large hospitals. Also, whatever he learned would be taught to other black doctors and interns through clinics and demonstrations.

All these things he could have explained. But he did not. He was never one to talk much about himself. The people close to him realized how much the situation over Provident had hurt and humiliated him. What hurt most was the thought that black people had begun to believe the gossipy remarks and insinuations that Dr. Hall and his followers continued to spread.

"Dr. Williams and his wife are snobs. They think they are better than the rest of us."

"Dr. Williams and his wife are trying to be white."

Sometimes, when Dr. Hall talked with groups, he would ask, "Do any dark-skinned people ever go to visit the Williams' home?"

Dr. Dan's actions did not help the situation. He had grown very serious and conservative. Now he dressed in dark suits and hats. He was never one to waste time in idle chit chat, and in recent years as his work multiplied, he seemed preoccupied most of the time. On the streets, people he met would have to speak twice before he recognized them.

Had Alice been like Theodocia, Dr. Hall's wife, she would have known how to speak up for her husband. But Alice had been brought up in protected seclusion by her mother. She knew how to treat the "correct" people, but never learned how to be friendly with the masses of poor folk. She lacked the warm, outgoing personality that would have won people to Dr. Dan's side.

Dr. Hall and his wife were the opposite. He was suave and a flashy dresser. He had a hearty laugh, a handshake, a joke to exchange with any group around him. He was never too busy to stop and exchange a bit of gossip.

Theodocia Hall, though not as daintily pretty as Alice, was a striking woman. She, like her husband, was gay and breezy, willing to make friends with anyone who could help her husband's career.

Dr. Dan was caught in a web. He was a gentle man, a shy man. He could heal, and teach, and crusade. But nothing in his experience prepared him for the feud waged by Dr. Hall. He had spent the better part of his life crusading for better health for black people. Now his own race was turning against him.

Not all, but enough. The people of Chicago seemed to form two camps. Some were all for Dr. Dan. "He has dedicated his life to medicine and to helping poor people," these said.

The other side agreed with Dr. Hall. "Dr. Dan is disloyal and he has turned his back on his race," they declared. "He spends most of his time helping white people."

Families took sides. Harry Anderson and his new wife were loyal to Dr. Dan. On the other hand, Daniel Herbert Anderson, Dr. Dan's godson and namesake, turned against him. Dr. Anderson never forgave his godfather for taking Dr. Ulysses Grant Dailey as an assistant after he refused to take him.

Even on a national scale, people took sides.

Booker T. Washington sided with Dr. Hall. His famous personal secretary, Emmett Scott, remained loyal to Dr. Dan, who had once saved his life. When Scott became deathly ill, Dr. Dan had rushed to Tuskegee, performed the needed operation, and stayed with Scott until he was out of danger.

Brokenhearted by it all, Dr. Dan withdrew more and more unto himself. The loneliness that had marked his early life now returned. This was the real tragedy. At the height of his greatness in medicine, Dr. Dan lessened his public crusading. The hospitals he might have built, the scientific papers he might have written; all this was left undone. He began a period of semi self-exile.

The real loser was the world of medical science. In this arena, his reputation as a surgical genius was beyond question. Nothing could shake his solid place in the annals of surgery. The world had proof of this.

On the evening of November 13, 1913, a group of one hundred surgeons assembled in the Gold Room of Chicago's Congress Hotel. Some of Dr. Dan's old teachers were among them. Some of his schoolmates were there, and yes, some of his students.

Dr. Daniel Hale Williams was there too.

These doctors were being inducted as charter members into the American College of Surgeons.

This prestigious organization included only the most distinguished surgeons in the United States and Canada. Dr. Dan Williams was the only black surgeon invited to become a Fellow. For many years after this, the group discriminated against the black doctors who were qualified to become members.

It was a high honor, but as usual, Dr. Dan tried to think how he might use it to inspire black students. That night when he came home, he wrote a letter to Emmett Scott at Tuskegee. He asked Scott to place the story in the New York *Age,* the newspaper Booker T. Washington controlled. Perhaps the recognition would in some way assist others, he wrote. Despite all that had happened, he was constantly thinking of ways to advance the black race.

Other honors followed. Wilberforce University in Ohio conferred an honorary degree upon him. Later, Howard University honored him with another. Friends and doctors who admired and loved him, constantly gave gifts, birthday parties, and other tokens of high regard.

Dr. Dan continued his private practice and his work in hospitals—other than Provident. He withdrew from public crusading, but he never withdrew from educating and healing. Struggling students knew that they could come to him for advice and financial help. They knew that if they could not talk with him in person they could seek his advice through letters and he would answer them.

From this great surgeon students learned an unforgettable lesson. For a doctor, the art of healing must come first.

CHAPTER 15

A Time of Peace

It was a time of peace.

Dr. Daniel Hale Williams drove his green Model T Ford along the country roads of the Michigan north woods. Alice sat beside him. The days of the horse-drawn surreys were behind them. Dr. Dan had fallen in love with Henry Ford's invention and enjoyed driving a car.

It was the summer of 1922. World War I had ended. Fighting men had returned from Europe. America looked forward to the twentieth century as a time of peace and advancement.

Dr. Dan nosed the car toward Idlewild, a vacation retreat in Lake County, Michigan. Giant oak and pine trees stood like sentinels along the way to welcome the weary riders.

Dr. Dan had joined with several black business men to buy a tract of forested land and develop a vacation retreat. "This resort," Dr. Dan said, "must not be an ordinary summer resort. We must plan health and cultural activities for people who come. We must have famous visiting lecturers. . . ."

So they developed Idlewild. A clubhouse was

built, then a hotel. Later, individual homes were constructed.

Dr. Dan turned his Ford into the driveway of the new house he had built. On the graceful white arch above the gate they could see the name they had given their summer home: Oakmere. Around the white bungalow ran a low picket fence, similar to the fences he had known as a boy in Hollidaysburg.

The house was built on a knoll overlooking a small lake. To the left and right they could see the magnificent oaks and pines and silver birch trees. Inside the bungalow, a huge fireplace stretched across one side of the living room. Dr. Dan sawed and split all the logs they burned there. This helped to keep his muscles in tone, he told Alice.

The morning after he arrived, neighbors saw the doctor at work in his garden before dawn. His gardens at Oakmere were his pride and joy.

"He gives those plants the same tender care he gives his patients," his neighbors teased. The tulips, peonies, roses, and many exotic plants made Oakmere a showplace. Each time he came for vacation he brought new varieties of flowers and plants. He would experiment with them the way he conducted experiments in the medical laboratory. Samples of his prized plants and vegetables were shared proudly with friends at Idlewild and in Chicago.

In the afternoon Dr. Dan turned to another kind of recreation. He strolled down to the boat dock and diving pier. Neighborhood children stood together, grinning, to welcome him.

"What can I do for you?" Dr. Dan asked in a formal manner, teasing them with the twinkle in his eyes.

"You know," they called out. "You know, Dr. Dan."

A few minutes later Alice looked from the window and saw his speedboat, loaded with children, skimming across the water. Every day during his visit, the children came for their ride. "Dr. Dan loves children and flowers," was a familiar saying in Lake County.

On the afternoon of his second day of vacation Dr. Dan went out in his flat-bottomed rowboat. He took along a neighbor and favorite fishing partner, Charles Waddell Chestnut, the writer. Chestnut's short stories and novels had won him fame as one of the foremost American authors.

Later that evening, other neighbors joined Alice and Dr. Dan in the park across the road from his home. They talked and sang and watched the peaceful sunset over the lake.

In this manner the days flowed peacefully along. Idlewild had become Dr. Dan's salvation. The wind, the water, the green trees, and soft air refreshed his mind and calmed his nerves. Here, he could forget the sadness of leaving Provident, of having members of his race reject him. Here, he found peace. He came as often as he could.

At the end of a long vacation he and Alice packed their Ford with flowers and vegetables and headed back to Chicago. Dr. Dan resumed his hectic pace of caring for patients in his office and in the five hospitals he now served.

His career at St. Luke's proved to be the success he had hoped it would. When black patients came, he could arrange for them to have private rooms if they wished. If they preferred the wards, he could see that they were given courtesy and good care. The hospital eventually wanted to name a ward for the surgeon, but he refused to permit this. "I was afraid that this ward would become segregated," he told friends.

Dr. Dan kept up his interest in young black medical students. He would seek them out and learn their needs. If any of the students had difficulty with classes, they came to Dr. Dan. If they were hard-pressed to meet their bills, they knew of a great surgeon who had once faced the same problem. He always helped. Several times a year he and Alice would plan a big dinner for the black medical students of the city.

This gave him a chance to know them better.

In his years of withdrawal, his contact with students became his great joy. The unfortunate attack by Dr. Hall had made him a lonely person; true. On the other hand, the years had given him the wisdom that comes from long hours of lonely meditation. He knew how to advise young people.

151

He gained the wisdom to look upon the death of loved ones as a transition as inevitable and beautiful as fall and winter. He could accept it when his sister Florence, always his favorite, died suddenly, and Sally's death followed soon after. His mother had died earlier from a sudden stroke. Now only Dr. Dan, Ann, and Alice were left.

Dr. Dan had the wisdom to face his wife's illness when she became a victim of Parkinson's disease. This chronic nervous disorder made her a cripple, confined to a wheelchair. His strength became her strength and Alice took the change with graceful acceptance. "She is so brave," her friends said. Dr. Dan took her for lengthy visits to Oakmere where she, too, found peace.

Alice Williams died in 1924.

For her brief memorial service, a friend read a poem which Alice had marked in a copy of one of her books. The verse was her favorite, "Crossing the Bar" by Alfred Lord Tennyson.

> But such a tide of moving seems asleep,
> Too full for sound and foam,
> When that which drew from out the boundless deep
> Turns again home.

A year later Dr. Dan grieved over the death of Harry Anderson. The affection between the two men had never wavered. Dr. Dan pleaded with Dr.

Bert Anderson to let him have the honor of placing the headstone on Anderson's grave. His godson refused. He still held resentment against Dr. Dan for not making him an assistant.

There was still medicine. One friend said, "From the time Dr. Dan became a doctor the greatest interest in his life was medicine." He continued to practice even when he developed diabetes and his own health began to fail. There were times when he was unable to drive himself, but he had someone to drive him to see his patients.

He never lost his crusading spirit for building hospitals. After a stroke confined him to a wheelchair, he would sit with his old friend, Dr. Frank Billings, and help plan a new interracial hospital for Chicago.

Another doctor who visited him often and sought his counsel was his former assistant, Dr. Ulysses Grant Dailey. Encouraged by Dr. Dan, Dr. Dailey had studied in Europe and returned to Chicago to open his own private hospital. Dr. Dan talked with him about Provident, and how the hospital was declining.

"Go back one day," he urged Dr. Dailey, "Go back and build Provident into the place it should be."

His former student promised to go back. He did.

Throughout his years of self-exile, Dr. Dan remained a great letter writer. As long as he could hold a pen he wrote to advise doctors and to help plan hospitals.

A longtime friend, Dr. Henry Minton, was director of Mercy Hospital in Philadelphia. The hospital was established by black doctors to care for their patients. From his wheelchair, Dr. Dan wrote Dr. Minton that he was sending his personal collection of books to build a library for the hospital. "It only takes a small room and some chairs and shelves," he wrote, "but why not a pretty room neatly furnished. It will add so much to your hospital."

When Dr. Dan sent the books, he wrote of his feelings in parting with his collection of more than forty years. "I part with them with a love which cannot be expressed in words. Like soldiers they have helped lead the way in many battles which seemed almost impregnable."

Like his father before him, Daniel Hale Williams crusaded for the advancement of black people until the end of his life.

The final peace came at Oakmere on Tuesday, August 4, 1931. Newspapers flashed the sad news to the world.

One of the most beautiful tributes to the surgeon was written by an editor who was his neighbor at Idlewild. It was printed in the *Lake County Star.*

"Modest, retiring, unassuming, he found his little world here full of reverent, loving friends. To the children he was 'Dr. Dan' and a friend, even though regarded awesomely as a miracle man. . . ."

"Like many other truly great men he found peace, solace and instruction in nature. He loved his flowers and his garden was filled with lovely native and exotic plants. He loved the woods and waters and the living things in them. . . "

Dr. Dan's will reflected his lifelong interests. He remembered his family, making provision for the care of his sisters, Ann and Alice. He also provided for the care of Price's children, especially for a daughter, Ada Blanche Zaratt, who gave up her home in Puerto Rico to come and care for him during his final illness.

He remembered friends. One bequest went to Ida Williams Lord, step-sister to Carrie Jacobs Bond. He always remembered Ida as the girl who had loved him in Janesville.

Most of his money went to the causes for which he had crusaded—the YMCA, the NAACP, Howard and Meharry Medical Colleges. Of all the medical schools founded to educate black doctors, these are the two that survived. They are the two with which Dr. Dan is closely associated.

Because of the feud with Dr. Hall and Dr. Dan's withdrawal from public life, his achievements were not widely publicized in the years following his death. When visitors went to Provident there was no reminder that Dr. Dan had founded the hospital. His picture had been stored in the basement. Since

Dr. Dan never wrote his life story, there was little in print about him. Would the second part of Dr. Hall's prophesy come true? Would Dr. Dan be forgotten?

Never. This has all changed. The world began to remember the many contributions he made to medicine. Because of his daring in surgery and his crusading in building hospitals, health care is better today for all people.

His editor-neighbor in Lake County knew him well. He ended his memorial tribute with an invitation for everyone to know Dr. Daniel Hale Williams better.

"To have known him was a pleasure—to know him intimately was a priceless privilege."

Selected Readings

Adams, Russell L. *Great Negroes Past and Present*. Chicago: Afro-American Publishing, 1964.

Brackett, Jeffrey. *The Negro in Maryland*. Baltimore: Johns Hopkins, 1899.

Buckler, Helen. *Daniel Hale Williams, Negro Surgeon*. 2d ed. New York: Pitman Publishing Corp., 1968.

Bullock, Ralph. *In Spite of Handicaps*. New York: Association Press, 1927.

Clapsesattle, Helen. *The Doctors Mayo*. Minneapolis: University of Minnesota Press, 1941.

Cobb, W. Montague. "Dr. Daniel H. Williams—Pioneer and Innovator." *Journal of the National Medial Association,* October, 1931.

"Daniel Hale Williams." Typed manuscript in Schomberg Collection, New York City.

Dictionary of American Biography. 21 vols. New York: Charles Scribner's Sons, 1928–36. Article on Daniel Hale Williams by James M. Phalen.

Gaines, Irene M., and U. G. Dailey. "Dr. Dan Williams." *The Crisis,* January, 1932.

Haber, Louis. *Black Pioneers of Science and Invention*. New York: Harcourt Brace Jovanovich, 1970.

Haskin, Sara Estelle, ed. *The Upward Climb*. "Another Daniel Who Dared." by Rebecca Caudill. Council for Home Missions, Methodist Episcopal Church, South, 1927.

Hughes, Langston. *Famous American Negroes*. New York: Dodd, Mead, 1954.

Jackson, Chevalier. *The Life of Chevalier Jackson.* New York: Macmillan, 1938.

Link, Eugene P. "The Civil Rights Activities of Three Great Negro Physicians, 1840-1940." *Journal of Negro History,* July 1967.

Meriwether, Louise. *Dr. Daniel Hale Williams.* Englewood Cliffs, N.J., Prentice-Hall, 1972.

Morais, Herbert M. *The History of the Negro in Medicine.* International Library of Negro Life and History, 2d ed. Vol. 3. Washington, D.C.: Association for the Study of Negro Life and History, 1967.

Moxcey, Mary, "Daniel Hale Williams" in *Rising Above Color,* ed. Philip Lotz. New York: Association Press, 1943.

Redding J. Saunders. *The Lonesome Road.* Garden City, N.Y.: Doubleday & Co., 1938.

Fenderson, Lewis H. *Daniel Hale Williams, Open-Heart Doctor.* New York, McGraw-Hill Book Company, 1971.

Klein, Aaron E. *The Hidden Contributors, Black Scientists and Inventors in America.* Garden City, New York, Doubleday & Co., 1971.

Reitzes, Dietrich. *Negroes and Medicine.* Cambridge, Mass: Harvard University Press, 1958.

Rhodes, Juliana Willis. "Daniel Hale Williams." *Negro History Bulletin,* May, 1942.

Riley, Elihu S. *The Ancient City, A History of Anne Arundel County.* Annapolis, Maryland, 1887.

Rollins, Charlemae. *They Showed the Way.* New York: Thomas Y. Crowell Co., 1964.

Stratton, Madeline. *Negroes Who Helped Build America.* Lexington, Mass: Ginn and Co., 1965.

Wisconsin, A Guide to the Badger State. New York: Hastings House and the Wisconsin Library Association, 1941.

Wright, James M. *The Free Negro in Maryland,* 1634-1860. New York: Columbia University Press, 1921.

SELECTED READINGS

Newspapers:
Chicago Defender
New York Herald Tribune
Baltimore Sunpapers
Lake County Star
Daily Inter-Ocean, Saturday, July 22, 1893.
Afro-American
Magazines:
Ebony, March, 1968.
Negro Digest, February, 1944.
The Daniel Hale Williams Papers. Moorland-Spingarn Research Center, Howard University, Washington, D.C.